800 AIR FRYER RECIPES COOKBOOK

Complete Air Fryer Cookbook with Easy & Delicious Recipes for Beginners & Advanced Users.

BY

CLARA MILES

ISBN: 978-1-952504-61-7

COPYRIGHT © 2020 by CLARA MILES

All rights reserved. This book is copyright protected and it's for personal use only. Without the prior written permission of the publisher, no part of this publication should be reproduced, distributed, or transmitted in any form or by any means, including photocopying, recording, or other electronic or mechanical methods.

This book is sold with the idea that the author is not needed to render accounting, officially permitted, or otherwise, qualified services. It's recommended to seek for the services of a legal or professional, a practiced individual in the profession if advice is needed.

DISCLAIMER

The information written in this publication is geared for educational and entertainment purposes only. Concerted efforts have been made towards providing accurate, up to date and reliable complete information. The information in this book is true and complete to the best of our knowledge.

Neither the publisher nor the author takes any responsibility for any possible consequences of reading or enjoying the recipes in this book. The author and publisher disclaim any liability in connection with the use of information contained in this book. Under no circumstance will any legal responsibility or blame be apportioned against the author or publisher for any reparation, damages, or monetary loss due to the information herein, either directly or indirectly.

Table of Contents

INTRODUCTION 10

Meaning of Air Fryer 10

Benefits of Cooking with an Air Fryer 11

How the Air Fryer Works 13

How to Use the Air Fryer 14

How to Clean the Air Fryer 16

How to Maintain the Air Fryer 18

Air Fryer Frequently Asked Questions & Answers 19

AIR FRYER BREAKFAST RECIPES 21

    Crispy Easy Bacon 21

    Peach Baked Oatmeal 22

    Breakfast Frittata 23

    Hard Boiled Eggs 24

    Banana Scones 25

    Classic Buttermilk Pancakes 26

    Dutch Baby Pancakes 27

    Baked Potatoes with Sour Cream and Chives 28

    Broccoli Cheese Crustless Quiche 29

    Crispy Baked Potatoes 30

    Cajun Chicken Wrap 31

    Sweet Potato Fries 32

    Blooming Onion 33

Mozzarella Sticks 35

Buddha Bowl 36

Avocado Fries 37

Honey Sriracha Glazed Meatballs 39

AIR FRYER POULTRY RECIPES 40

Chicken Parmesan 40

20 Minute Chicken Breast 41

Baked Chicken Drumsticks 42

Southern Fried Chicken without Buttermilk 43

Greek Chicken Wraps 44

Chicken Nuggets 45

Chicken Wings 46

Fried Chicken 47

Turkey Breast 48

Lemon Pepper Air Fryer Chicken Thighs 49

Pesto Chicken Pita 50

AIR FRYER FISH & SEAFOOD RECIPES 51

Fish Sticks 51

Easy Salmon 52

Salmon Bok Choy 53

Spicy Crab Dip 55

Gorton's Fish Fillets 56

Salt and Pepper Shrimp 57

Spicy Garlic Prawn 58

King Prawns 59

White Fish with Garlic and Lemon 60

Garlic Parmesan Air Fried Shrimp 61

Shrimp Fried Rice 62

Shrimp Scampi 64

AIR FRYER BEEF & PORK RECIPES 65

Kenyan Braised Collard Greens and Ground Beef 65

Italian Beef Hoagies 66

Bacon Burger Bites 68

Beef Empanadas 69

Beef Jerky 70

Pork Chops 71

Roast Lamb 72

Roast Pork 73

Garlic Lovers Roast Beef 74

Cajun Pork Burgers 75

AIR FRYER MAIN MEAL RECIPES 76

Lemon Pepper Chicken 76

Thai Salmon Patties 77

Fish Finger Sandwich 78

Hot Dog 79

Tandoori Paneer Naan Pizza 80

Meatball Parmesan Casserole 81

Air Fryer Tofu 82

Sweet Chili Fish Wraps 83

Baked Tofu Steaks with Lemon and Garlic 84

Smoky Bean Chili 85

AIR FRYER EGG RECIPES 86

Herb Zucchini and Kale Egg Bake 86

Baked Egg Cups with Spinach and Cheese 87

Broccoli Cheese Chicken Egg Rolls 88

Quinoa Egg Muffins 89

Cheesy Egg Taco-Dilla 90

Scotch Eggs 91

Bacon And Cheese Egg Muffins 92

Sheet Pan Eggs 93

Baked Eggs 94

AIR FRYER SIDE DISH RECIPES 95

Maple Butter Acorn Squash 95

Maple Cinnamon Roasted Butternut Squash 96

Coconut Cranberry Muffins 97

Sweet Potato 98

Mushroom with Bruschetta and Goat Cheese 99

Balsamic Roasted Brussels Sprouts 100

Spaghetti Squash 101

Honey Roasted Carrots 102

Nashville Hot Chicken 103

Breaded Mushrooms 105

Frozen Curly Fries 106

AIR FRYER VEGAN & VEGETARIAN RECIPES 107

Sticky Pumpkin Wedges 107

Flourless Broccoli Cheese Quiche 108

Black Bean Burger 109

Chocolate Chip Zucchini Bread 110

Fried Green Tomatoes 111

Rutabaga Fries 112

Zucchini Vegetarian Meatballs 113

Meatless Monday Thai Veggie Bites 114

Meatless Monday Veggie Bake Cakes 116

Vegan Veggie Balls 117

Pumpkin French Toast 118

Pumpkin Bread 119

AIR FRYER BURGER RECIPES 120

Bunless Burgers 120

Leftover Turkey Burgers 121

Juicy Cheeseburgers 122

Lentil Burgers 123

Falafel Burger 124

Hamburgers 125
KFC Zinger Chicken Burger 126
Portobello Burger with Basil Pesto-mayo 127
Gourmet Blue Cheese Burgers 128
Lamb Burgers 129

AIR FRYER APPETIZER RECIPES 130

Asparagus Fries 130
Banana Bread 131
Cheesy Garlic Bread 133
Corn Nuts 134
Air Fryer Donut 135
Shishito Peppers 136
Spicy Roasted Peanuts 137
Tempura Veggies 138
Potato Hay 139
Honey Garlic Chicken Wings 140
Fried Pickles 141
Chinese Garlic Chicken 142

AIR FRYER DESSERT RECIPES 143

Cashew Chocolate Brownies 143
Apple Pie Egg Rolls 144
Chocolate Chip Oatmeal Cookies 145
Apple Chips 146

Zebra Butter Cake 147

Strawberry Cheesecake Egg Rolls 148

Campfire Nutella Smores 149

Shortbread 150

Chocolate Cake 151

Midnight Nutella Banana Sandwich 152

Air Baked Molten Lava Cakes 153

INTRODUCTION

Meaning of Air Fryer

The world's market is trending with the Air Fryer as its popularity is gaining momentum. Beginners seek to know what an Air Fryer is. It is pertinent to know what a product is before buying it. An Air Fryer is a well-known kitchen unit that enables you to cook sumptuous fried foods like potato chips, fish, and pastries by hitting up air and circulate all around the food to give you a crispy result. In a more advanced way, Air Fryer can be said to be a compact kitchen unit which heat through convection to spread the air all over the food. There is a fan that rotates and move the air around the food placed in the Air Fryer cooking basket. With a result of less fat, it gives you a delicious meal with high level of crispiness.

Air Fryer is capable of cooking what a microwave can't cook perfectly well. What makes an Air Fryer unique is the ability to reheat previous night's French fries, warms, fries and make it crispy. The Air Fryer was designed as a multi-purpose kitchen unit that doesn't only use super-heated air with small or no oil but can also cook delicious and sumptuous foods and can also hydrate your fruit, veggies and meat without all fats and calories. The whirlwind of super-heated air gives your food a crispy taste without adding all the fats and calories.

Benefits of Cooking with an Air Fryer

Air Fryer has gained popularity and great momentum due to its uniqueness, versatility and durability. There are lots of health and social benefits for both beginners and old Air Fryer users. Below are some of the benefits that the users can enjoy without regretting purchasing the multi-purpose kitchen appliance.

1. **You can cook frozen foods in the Air Fryer.**

Yes, fresh and frozen foods can be cooked in the Air Fryer. You can even reheat leftovers. Some brand of Air Fryers comes with components like grill pan, cooking rack etc. You can cook different things at the same time using the dividable cooking basket.

2. **Air Fryer is easy for clean-up.**

Some people feel reluctant cleaning their cooking gadgets after every use may be because they are difficult to clean. Some Air Fryer parts are dishwasher safe. You only need to wash the basket and cooking pan. The appliance is very easy for a full clean up and doesn't involve difficult task.

3. **Air Fryer uses hot air and circulate all-round the food not large amount of oil.**

There is an element that heat up and ventilate air around the food with or without the use of oil. It doesn't require that the food should be sunk into large hot oil instead the heated air circulates some oil droplets to coat the food thereby cooking the food to your desired consistency. The Air Fryer can brown the food if desired unlike the microwave.

4. **There are no potential fire hazards like hot air over an open flame.**

Lots of cases have been on the news about fire outbreak globally relating to cooking with hot oil. The good news about Air Fryer is that it doesn't splatter hot oil on both your hands and forearms. This can only happen when the Air Fryer is faulty. When the Air Fryer is working properly, there is no potential hazard like hot oil over the open flame. The temperature of the Air Fryer is simple to set alongside with time.

5. **Air Fryer reduces exposure to toxic acryl-amide formation.**

Research indicates that acryl-amide formulation takes place during high-heat cooking and possibly can lead to kidney cancer. Instead of deep frying, Air Fryer improves healthy eating through the removal of fat and oil. Through this process, the level of your exposure to acryl-amide will be greatly reduced.

6. **Air Fryer helps in cooking foods that are in limited quantities.**

The Air Fryer is a good option if what you want to cook is in limited quantities. Most brands of the Air Fryer can cook a chicken pot pie, roasted asparagus or French fries. Die to its size, the Air Fryer may not be able to cook a whole dinner for a family that is up to 4 members.

7. **Air frying is more preferably than deep frying in terms of healthy food.**

Indeed, the food that is air-fried is a good alternative to food that is deep-fried. The Air Fryer is unique and people like it especially for the fact that air fried foods can reduce the amount of calories and fats in the nutritional composition of your food. Air-fried foods are lower in calories, fat and some harmful substance that are usually found in deep fried foods.

Those who are so desperate in losing weight without cutting down fried foods have the option to switch to Air Fried foods. It's a good choice for them. Despite these facts, eating air fried foods should be in moderation because excessive eating of air-fried foods can cause some health challenges.

8. **Air Fryer cooking time is faster than the traditional oven.**

The big traditional kitchen oven or the smaller toaster oven may take a longer cooking cycle compared to the Air Fryer which is faster and still gives crispy meals. For instance, if you want to cook Brussels sprouts, Air Fryer takes about 30 minutes to completely cook the food. However, microwave could be faster than the Air Fryer but the air frying process is simple to understand.

9. **Air Fryer is good for picky eaters.**

Air Fryer is a good option for picky vegetable eaters at home. Air Fryer can help to crisp up veggies and make them tastier. The result is always delicious and sumptuous meals.

10. **Air Fryer can substitute frying of foods.**

Foods cooked in the Air Fryer are healthier than foods that were fried with oil. The continuous use of Air Fryer to cook food can result in reduction of fat calories by 75%. Frying food sometimes require recycling the used oil and the oil most times bring out unpleasant smell for some days.

How the Air Fryer Works

There is an element that heat up and ventilate air around the food with or without the use of oil. It however needs a tablespoon of oil in order to get the same taste compared to deep fried foods. Knowing how the Air Fryer works is very important as it may contribute to the longevity and durability of the appliance. Air Fryer works perfectly well by heating up air and circulate it all around the food.

Air Fryer users especially the beginners have to get themselves familiarized with the appliance and how it works. It has various buttons depending on the models. You have to be familiarized with these buttons as this will also help to make you really understand how the Air Fryer works.

However, Air Fryer does not really fry food. The food is place in the cooking basket and then the Air Fryer through its heating element heat up and ventilates air around the food. The food in the basket is browned and cooked through the force of the air which produces convection. When the heat sums up to 3200F, foods like frozen chicken tenders or French fries will turn to brown.

How to Use the Air Fryer

Here are some of the main points on how to use an Air Fryer:

1. **Flip and Toss the food for proper doneness.**

This is very important when you are cooking in the Air Fryer. You are required to flip or turn over to the other side before you remove the food from heat. This is to enable the food to be properly cooked on both sides. Some foods may stick to the Air Fryer basket thereby blocking the free flow of hot air. Flipping the food is very important and needed to be done if you must achieve optimum result.

Moreover, it is advisable to flip over the food halfway through the cooking cycle and then continue cooking to complete the stipulated cooking time. Some foods require that you flip and turn the food 2 times before the cooking time is over. The easiest way to flip the food is to use a pair of tongs to rotate the food from up to down and vice versa.

2. **Always keep your Air Fryer clean.**

Cleaning the appliance after every use is one of the good measures for durability of the product. When food residue is stock up in the cooking basket and other parts, you need to give the unit a thorough cleaning to avoid some unpleasant smell coming out from the remains of foods.

3. **Spray the basket with cooking spray.**

The reason why the Air Fryer cooking basket needs to be spray with cooking oil spray is because some foods with breadcrumb coating do stick to the basket while cooking. In order to get rid of this sticking, the basket needs to be spray with cooking oil spray before the cooking commence. Make sure the basket is sprits with cooking oil spray. For instance, if you are cooking foods like fish, it may likely stick to the basket so spraying with cooking oil spray is highly recommended.

4. **Try not to overcrowd the Air Fryer while cooking.**

According to the manufacturer's Instructions, it is warned that you do not overcrowd the cooking basket. This is because of the size of the basket. On this note, you are advised to cook foods that are much in 2 or 3 batches. If you Over crowd the cooking basket, they may not be enough space for the appliance to circulate air therefore, the food might not be properly cooked. The Air Fryer always comes with a manual which will also indicate how to fill the cooking basket. When the basket is filled up or overcrowded, the food will not evenly be cooked on all sides.

5. **Divide the food and cook in Batches.**

This has to do with the size of the Air Fryer. It is one of the manufacturer's Instructions not to overcrowd the Air Fryer basket. You have to cook in 2 or 3 batches depending on the quantity of the food. If you have visitors and you want to serve them at the same time, you can keep the first batch somewhere warm until you complete all the batches and then serve them all at once.

6. **Dry Your Food before cooking.**

Crispiness and brown food are the watchwords for using an Air Fryer. Browning is synonymous to caramelization which is the reason why carbohydrate will get darkened when heated above 300ºF. Crispiness comes in due to the drying of the surface of the food. The hot oil which the food is immersed in to boils the moisture away from the surface of the food thereby making it crispy. Base on this fact, the more your food gets dried up when you start to cook it, the better result you will get from the Air Fryer by crisping the outer part of your food. To dry the food, it is advised you use paper towels to pat dry them.

How to Clean the Air Fryer

Cleaning the appliance after every use is one of the good measures for durability of the product. When food residue is stock up in the cooking basket and other parts, you need to give the unit a thorough cleaning to avoid some unpleasant smell coming out from the remains of foods. Begin the cleaning process by unplugging the unit from power source; allow it to cool off if it is still hot. This may take about 30 minutes in order to align with room temperature. Follow these simple steps below:

1. **Clean the outside using damp cloth.**

Use lint free cloth damp in hot water in order to remove finger prints and food residue from the outside of the Air Fryer. Use the damp cloth to wipe down all the exterior surfaces.

2. **Remove the cooking basket and pan.**

The main purpose of doing this is to turn the unit upside down to enable your hand reach the heating element and clean it thoroughly. The heating element sits above the basket and pan that is the reason you have to remove the basket and pan and flip the unit upside down. When you remove the basket and pan, keep it aside. With your two hands to rotate the unit and set the unit on a flat surface let the cleaning begins.

In the other hand, there are some components that require you to wash after every use; some need to be washed occasionally while some need deep cleaning.

A. **What to Wash after Each Use.**

The basket, tray and pan need to be washed with soap and warm water after every use. There are 2 ways to do the washing. First is by hand and another one is by dishwasher. If you dislike hand washing, you can opt for the dishwasher. Most Air Fryer models come with dishwasher safe pieces. After the wash, make sure to dry all the components before fixing them back. In case the cooking pan is filled with grease, what you need to do is to soak in warm and soapy water for about 20 minutes. Remove and wash thoroughly.

B. **What to Wash Occasionally.**

Air Fryer makes use of little oil for its crispy result. On this note, the exterior part of the unit only needs to be washed occasionally not regularly. This can be done by using a damp cloth to clean the outside of the Air Fryer after every use. Please confirm that you unplug the unit before you begin the cleaning process. If it is still hot, please allow it to cool off for sometimes.

C. **Deep cleaning the Air Fryer.**

In order to deep clean the Air Fryer, the first thing you should do is to pour baking soda solution onto the heating element. Turn the unit upside down and use a spray bottle to sprits the solution on the heating element. Keep aside for 2 minutes. Turn the Air Fryer right side up and set aside for 30 minutes. If there is more stubborn residue, repeat the above steps. Put water into the pan. You can begin with a clean pan to avoid more food residue to spread around the Air Fryer. Dry and replace the pan and basket into the Air Fryer after the washing is done.

Run the Air Fryer at 392OF for 20 minutes to get rid of any remaining residue. Connect the appliance back into power source. Running the unit this way will ensure the moisture and baking soda solution will help get rid of sticky spot. Get rid of the water and residue found in the basket.

How to Maintain the Air Fryer

Acquiring the Air Fryer could be easy but maintaining the appliance is what pose serious attention and focus on the global scene. Do not use metal tools or steel wire sponges to clean your Air Fryer. This is also applicable while doing preparations for cooking your food. You don't need to use metal object. You may use the dishwasher to do the washing instead of doing hand washing. You always need to remove the pan and cooking basket to wash them and then fix them back. In most cases, liquid fats drip out easily. When this happens, use a plastic utensil to scoop out the solid fats. Avoid using metals while cleaning the Air Fryer because the non-stick coating on the pan might be scratched.

Frequent checking of the cords before every use to ensure they aren't faulty. A faulty cord can damage the whole appliance and can pose a serious injury or death. Never manage any damaged cord, replace with new cord when you find out that the cord is faulty.

Another maintenance tips you should consider is inspecting the appliance and making sure it is clean before you commence any cooking. Some dust might have covered the unit if it has been long you last used the appliance so make sure you get rid of the dust before you start using it. If there is any food residue, clean it before you starts using it.

Moreover, it is advisable to place the appliance in an upright position on a balanced or flat surface and it should not be placed close to the wall. This is because the appliance requires the minimum space of 4 inches behind and above it for proper ventilation of hot air. Overheat may occur if the appliance is placed close to the wall or another appliance.

Air Fryer Frequently Asked Questions & Answers

1. **My Air fryer is having difficulty to start. What could be the cause?**

If this problem occurs, it is a power problem so to be serviced. Seek for the attention of a repairer to check the power problem. You have to test and try to solve the problem by yourself first before you put a call to the manufacturer or a repairer. Make sure the appliance is properly plugged to power source. If there's any damaged cord, replace with new one or if there's any components that is faulty, do not manage it instead replace with new one.

2. **I'm I expected to clean the Air Fryer after every use?**

Yes, you should clean the Air Fryer after every use but you need to allow it to be cool enough to handle with your hands. Remove the components and give it a thorough wash by placing them in the dishwasher with warm soapy water. Pat dry all the components very well before fixing it back.

3. **Cooking with the Air Fryer, is the food tasty and delicious?**

The answer is yes. Air Fryer gives delicious and sumptuous meal provided the intended food is tasty by itself.

4. **What should I do to prevent food from sticking to my Air Fryer basket?**

If you are cooking food like fish or chicken, they are prone to sticking in the cooking basket. What you need to do is to spray the basket with any cooking spray. This will ease the removal of the food when they are done.

5. **What quantity of food should I place on the cooking basket?**

The best option is to use your own judgment. It is not good to Over crowd the Air Fryer cooking basket in order to allow free flow of hot air around the food. The quantity depends on the size of your Air Fryer. Divide the food and cook in batches if they are much. The second batch should be checked for doneness frequently because the appliance was already hot after the first batch.

6. **Is there any extra components I need to purchase?**

Some models of the appliance come with attached components like pans and racks. These attachments could be useful for some specified reasons. The basket is capable of giving you a complete cooking cycle without using the extra components.

7. What causes my Air Fryer to bring out unpleasant smell?

When you finish cooking and fail to clean the appliance, there's bound to be some leftovers on the unit. When the unit is left unclean, the leftover will bring out an unpleasant odor. Make sure you clean the appliance after every use to avoid the odor. There are some instances where the odour still persist even after you might have cleaned the appliance after use, you have to soak the pan and basket in a dishwasher with warm soapy water for about 40 minutes and the wash it again. If the smell still persists, use lemon and rub it all over the pan and basket. This should be the final solution to the problem.

8. What causes my Air Fryer to peel?

If you want to place the basket in the Air Fryer and you mistakenly scratch the appliance or you wrongly place the basket, the hot air while cooking may cause peeling or bubbling to occur because Air Fryer components are covered with a non-stick coating. The coating is not harmful to your health but try and replace any component that peel.

9. Sliding the pan into the Air Fryer is difficult, what is the cause?

This is simply caused by Overcrowding the basket with too much food. It is always advisable to cook for in batches if they are really much. When you have done this, make sure you properly insert the pan correctly. When it clicks then you know you have fix it properly.

10. My food is not cooked properly, what causes that?

If you noticed this problem, it may be that you overcrowded the Air Fryer cooking basket with much food giving the appliance very little space for it to circulate hot air around the food. What you need to do is to cook in batches if you have enough quantity of food to place in the Air Fryer basket.

AIR FRYER BREAKFAST RECIPES

Crispy Easy Bacon

Preparation Time: 2 minutes

Cooking Time: 12 minutes

Total Time: 14 minutes

Servings: 6

Calories: 183 kcal

Ingredients:

- 12 slices of streaky bacon smoked

Cooking Instructions:

1. Begin by Preheating the Air Fryer to 350°F and use a single layer to arrange the bacon in the Air Fryer cooking basket.

2. The 12 slices may require 2 batches depending on your Air Fryer size.

3. Cook in the Air Fryer for up to 12 minutes and make sure you turn the bacon halfway through the cooking time.

4. Serve and enjoy!!!

Peach Baked Oatmeal

Preparation Time: 15 minutes

Cooking Time: 50 minutes

Total Time: 1 hour 5 minutes

Servings: 8

Calories: 237 kcal

Ingredients:

- ½ Tsp. ground ginger
- 2 Cups of almond milk
- 3 Cups of rolled oats
- 2 Tsp. baking powder
- 1 Tsp. cinnamon
- ½ Tsp. nutmeg
- ½ Cup of maple syrup
- 2 Eggs
- 3 Peaches
- ¼ Cup of sliced almonds

Cooking Instructions:

1. Begin by Preheating the Air Fryer to 350°F and rub oil on the casserole dish.

2. Merge together the oats, baking powder, almond milk, spices, maple syrup and eggs. Make sure you stir thoroughly.

3. Put the peaches and pour the mixture you have gotten into the already oiled casserole and place almond slices on top.

4. Lay them in the Air Fryer and bake for up to 50 minutes. Top with greek yogurt, fresh peaches and maple syrup.

5. Serve and enjoy!!!

Breakfast Frittata

Preparation Time: 10 minutes

Cooking Time: 16 minutes

Total Time: 26 minutes

Servings: 4

Calories: 147 kcal

Ingredients:

- 4 Mushrooms sliced
- 3 Grape tomatoes cherry tomatoes, sliced into 2
- 4 Eggs
- 3 Tbsp. heavy cream double cream
- 4 Tbsp. grated cheddar cheese
- 4 Tbsp. chopped spinach
- 2 Tbsp. fresh chopped herbs you like
- 1 Green onion sliced
- Salt

Cooking Instructions:

1. Begin by Preheating the Air Fryer to 350°F and lay parchment paper on the baking pan you want to use. Wet the pan with oil and then keep aside.

2. Merge together the cream, and the remaining ingredients into a small mixing bowl. Mix the mixture thoroughly.

3. Take the oiled baki pan and pour the mixture into it and lay the pan in the Air Fryer cooking basket and then bake for up to 16 minutes.

4. Serve and enjoy!!!

Hard Boiled Eggs

Preparation Time: 1 minute

Cooking Time: 16 minutes

Total Time: 17 minutes

Servings: 2

Calories: 125 kcal

Ingredients:

- 4 Large Eggs

Cooking Instructions:

1. Begin by Preheating the Air Fryer to 250°F. Set in the Air Fryer basket and place the eggs on the top.

2. Cook for up to 16 minutes. When the cooking time is up, remove the eggs into a cool clean water and peel off when it is cool.

3. Serve and enjoy!!!

Banana Scones

Preparation Time: 5 minutes

Cooking Time: 12 minutes

Total Time: 17 minutes

Servings: 2

Calories: 184 kcal

Ingredients:

- 2 packages Jiffy Banana Muffin mix
- ¼ Cup of butter
- ½ Cup of sour cream
- ½ Cup of all-purpose flour

Cooking Instructions:

1. Begin by Preheating the Air Fryer to 350°F. in a medium mixing bowl, merge together the banana muffin mix, flour, butter and sour cream. Mix thoroughly.

2. Make the mixture into mold and try to press the ends to be stronger. Are them in the Air Fryer and cook for up to 12 minutes.

3. Shake the Air the Fryer after the cooking time and cook again for about 2 minutes. Flip unto a serving plate.

4. Serve and enjoy!!!

Classic Buttermilk Pancakes

Preparation Time: 10 minutes

Cooking Time: 10 minutes

Total Time: 20 minutes

Servings: 2 dozen

Calories: 193 kcal

Ingredients:

- 2 Tsp. baking powder
- 1 Tsp. salt
- 2 Cups of all-purpose flour
- 2 Tbsp. sugar
- 2 Eggs
- 2 Cups of buttermilk
- ¼ Cup of milk
- ¼ Melted butter

Cooking Instructions:

1. Begin by Preheating the Air Fryer to 350°F.

2. Merge together the flour, sugar, baking powder, eggs, buttermilk, milk, butter and salt in a large mixing bowl. Give it a thorough stir.

3. Wet the Air Fryer tray with olive oil, spoon 3 Tbsp. of the prepared flour mixture onto the tray.

4. Cook in the Air Fryer at 320°F for 5 minutes shaking the unit halfway through the cooking time.

5. Serve and enjoy!!!

Dutch Baby Pancakes

Preparation Time: 5 minutes

Cooking Time: 8 minutes

Total Time: 13 minutes

Servings: 8

Calories: 148 kcal

Ingredients:

- ½ Tsp. salt
- 4 Tbsp. butter (melted)
- 4 Large eggs
- 1 Cup of milk
- 1 Tsp. vanilla extract
- 1 Tbsp. sugar
- 1 Cup of flour

Cooking Instructions:

1. Begin by Preheating the Air Fryer to 350°F.

2. Merge together the eggs, milk, salt and 2 Tbsp. of butter, vanilla extract, sugar and flour in a large mixing bowl. Give it a thorough mixing.

3. Wet your cooking pan with the melted butter and fill the pan with the above mixture. Place it on the Air Fryer.

4. Cook at 330°F for 5 minutes, after this time flip over and cook for another 3 minutes. Flip onto a serving plate, top with fresh berries.

5. Serve and enjoy!!!

Baked Potatoes with Sour Cream and Chives

Preparation Time: 5 minutes

Cooking Time: 38 minutes

Total Time: 43 minutes

Servings: 4

Calories: 281 kcal

Ingredients:

- 2 Tsp. olive oil
- 4 Russet potatoes, rinsed
- ½ Cup of sour cream
- 3 Tbsp. diced chives

Cooking Instructions:

1. Begin by Preheating the Air Fryer to 350°F and then sprinkle oil all over the potatoes.

2. Arrange them in the Air Fryer and cook at 400°F for up to 38 minutes. Cut the potatoes open, and pour in Tbsp. of sour cream, and chives.

3. Serve and enjoy!!!

Broccoli Cheese Crustless Quiche

Preparation Time: 15 minutes

Cooking Time: 40 minutes

Total Time: 55 minutes

Servings: 8

Calories: 162 kcal

Ingredients:

- 1 Cup of milk
- 1 Head broccoli, chopped
- 6 Large eggs
- 1 Cup of cheese
- ¼ Tsp. salt

Cooking Instructions:

1. Begin by Preheating the Air Fryer to 350°F. Beat the eggs into a large glass measuring cup and add all the ingredients.

2. Pour the mixture into a greased pie plate checking for even distribution of the Broccoli. Place in the Air Fryer and bake for 40 minutes.

3. Serve and enjoy!!!

Crispy Baked Potatoes

Preparation Time: 5 minutes

Cooking Time: 45 minutes

Total Time: 50 minutes

Servings: 3

Calories: 194 kcal

Ingredients:

- 3 Russet potatoes, stubbed and pat dried
- 2 Tsp. oil
- Salt

Cooking Instructions:

1. Begin by Preheating the Air Fryer to 390°F. Poke a hole on the potatoes using fork, season with salt and apply oil.

2. Arrange the potatoes in the Air Fryer cooking basket and bake for up to 30 minutes. Flip over and cook again for another 20 minutes.

3. Serve and enjoy!!!

Cajun Chicken Wrap

Preparation Time: 15 minutes

Cooking Time: 15 minutes

Total Time: 30 minutes

Servings: 6

Calories: 338 kcal

Ingredients:

- 2 Large chicken breasts
- 3 Tbsp. Cajun seasoning divided
- 2 Tbsp. olive oil
- 2 Bell peppers, sliced
- 1 Red onion, sliced
- 2 Cups of cherry tomatoes quartered
- 4 large tortillas

Cooking Instructions:

1. Begin by Preheating the Air Fryer to 390°F. Apply oil on the cooking pan, season the chicken with the Cajun seasoning and lay it on the pan.

2. Place it in the Air Fryer cooking basket and cook for up to 7 minutes. Get the chicken out from the pan into a bowl.

3. Dump in bell pepper and onion to the pan alongside with 1 1/2 Tbsp. of Cajun seasoning. Cook for extra 5 minutes. Dump in tomatoes and cook for 1 minute.

4. Put the chicken into the pan. Give it a nice mixing. Share it into your desired containers.

5. Serve and enjoy!!!

Sweet Potato Fries

Preparation Time: 10 minutes

Cooking Time: 10 minutes

Total Time: 20 minutes

Servings: 2

Calories: 221 kcal

Ingredients:

- 2 Tsp. olive oil
- ½ Tsp. kosher salt
- 2 Medium peeled sweet potatoes, sliced into small sizes
- ½ Tsp. garlic powder
- ¼ Tsp. sweet paprika
- Fresh black pepper

Cooking Instructions:

1. Begin by Preheating the Air Fryer to 400°F. Sprinkle oil on the Air Fryer cooking basket.

2. Apply oil into the potatoes and add salt, garlic powder, black pepper and paprika.

3. Arrange them in the Air Fryer and cook for 8 minutes. Shaking the Air Fryer halfway to the cooking time.

4. Serve and enjoy!!!

Blooming Onion

Preparation Time: 15 minutes

Cooking Time: 25 minutes

Total Time: 40 minutes

Servings: 4

Calories: 381 kcal

Ingredients:

- 1 Cup of breadcrumbs
- 2 Tsp. paprika
- 1 Large yellow onion
- 3 Large eggs
- 1 Tsp. garlic powder
- 1 Tsp. onion powder
- 1 Tsp. kosher salt
- 3 Tbsp. extra-virgin olive oil

For the Sauce:

- ⅔ Cup of mayonnaise
- 2 Tbsp. ketchup
- 1 Tsp. horseradish
- ½ Tsp. paprika
- ½ Tsp. garlic powder
- ¼ Tsp. dried oregano
- Kosher salt

Cooking Instructions:

1. Begin by Preheating the Air Fryer to 400°F. Trim out the onion stem, from the flat side cut an inch of 15 sections from the root down.

2. Do not completely cut them off. Separate the petals from the sections. Merge together eggs and a Tbsp. of water in a small mixing bowl.

3. Get another bowl and combine together spices and breadcrumbs. Dump onion into egg mixture and breadcrumb mixture respectively.

4. Sprinkle oil on the onion. Arrange the onion in the Air Fryer cooking basket and cook at 375°F for up to 25 minutes.

5. Merge together the mayonnaise, ketchup, horseradish, paprika, garlic powder, salt and dried oregano in a medium mixing bowl for the sauce.

6. Serve and enjoy!!!

Mozzarella Sticks

Preparation Time: 40 minutes

Cooking Time: 25 minutes

Total Time: 1 hour 5 minutes

Servings: 4

Calories: 271 kcal

Ingredients:

- 1 Large egg
- ¼ Cup of all-purpose flour
- 1 (12 Oz.) Package mozzarella cheese sticks, Halved
- ¼ Cup of mayonnaise
- ¼ Cup of fine, dry breadcrumbs
- ½ Tsp. onion powder
- ½ to Tsp. garlic powder
- 1 Cup of marinara sauce

Cooking Instructions:

1. Begin by Preheating the Air Fryer to 370°F. Lay the Halved sticks on a rimmed baking sheet lined with parchment paper. Gather the breading.

2. In a medium mixing bowl, combine together the mayonnaise and egg in a medium bowl.

3. Put the flour, breadcrumbs, onion, and garlic powder in a large bowl and thoroughly mix the mixture.

4. Coat the sticks in the egg and flour mixtures respectively. Place the stick on the baking sheet in the freezer for 10 minutes.

5. Remove and arrange in the Air Fryer and bake for 5 minutes in batches.

6. Serve and enjoy!!!

Buddha Bowl

Preparation Time: 15 minutes

Cooking Time: 20 minutes

Total Time: 35 minutes

Servings: 4

Calories: 496 kcal

Ingredients:

- 1 Red onion, chopped
- 2 Cups of brussels sprouts, halved
- ¾ Cup cooked quinoa
- 2 Large carrots, chopped
- 2 Tbsp. olive oil
- Salt
- Pepper
- 19 Oz. can of chickpeas
- Tahini Dressing:
- 2 Tsp. maple syrup
- 2 Tbsp. tahini
- 2 Tbsp. water
- 2 Tsp. lemon juice
- salt

Cooking Instructions:

1. Begin by Preheating the Air Fryer to 400°F. Share the cooked quinoa in 4 containers. Line a baking sheet with parchment and keep aside.

2. Merge together the carrots, onion, Brussels sprouts, olive oil, salt and pepper. Spread the mixture on the baking sheet and bake for up to 20 minutes.

3. Don't fail to stir it during halfway through the cooking time. You may now shake all tahini dressing ingredients together.

4. Share the chickpeas into the 4 containers alongside with veggies and tahini dressing sauce. Serve and enjoy!!!

Avocado Fries

Preparation Time: 15 minutes

Cooking Time: 8 minutes

Total Time: 23 minutes

Servings: 4

Calories: 271 kcal

Ingredients:

- 2 Avocados, cut into 8 wedges
- ¼ Tsp. kosher salt
- ½ Cup of all-purpose flour
- 1 ½ Tsp. black pepper
- 2 Large eggs
- 1 Tbsp. water
- ½ Cup of panko
- ¼ Cup of no-salt-added ketchup
- 2 Tbsp. canola mayonnaise
- 1 Tbsp. apple cider vinegar
- 1 Tbsp. Sriracha chili sauce

Cooking Instructions:

1. Begin by Preheating the Air Fryer to 400°F. In a small mixing bowl, combine together flour and pepper.

2. In another small mixing bowl, beat the egg into it and put the water. On a third small mixing bowl, put the panko.

3. Coat the avocado wedges with the flour, egg and panko mixture respectively shaking off the excesses. Finally coat the avocado with cooking spray.

4. Arrange the avocado in the Air Fryer cooking basket and bake at 400°F for up to 8 minutes.

5. Make sure to shake the avocado over halfway through the cooking time. Remove and apply salt.

6. Before the cooking time is up, merge together ketchup, mayonnaise, vinegar, and Sriracha in a small mixing bowl.

7. Serve and enjoy!!

Honey Sriracha Glazed Meatballs

Preparation Time: 15 minutes

Cooking Time: 25 minutes

Total Time: 40 minutes

Servings: 8

Calories: 215 kcal

Ingredients:

- For the meatballs:
- 2 Lbs. lean ground turkey
- 1 Cup of whole wheat panko breadcrumbs
- 2 Eggs
- ¼ Cup of green onions, chopped
- ½ Tsp. garlic powder
- ½ Tsp. salt
- ½ Tsp. black pepper
- For the sauce:
- ¼ Cup of Sriracha
- 3 Tbsp. soy sauce
- 3 Tbsp. rice vinegar
- 3 Tbsp. honey
- 1 Tbsp. grated fresh ginger
- 3 Cloves garlic, minced
- ½ Tsp. toasted sesame oil

Cooking Instructions:

1. Begin by Preheating the Air Fryer to 375°F. Merge together the turkey, breadcrumbs, eggs, green onions, garlic powder, salt and pepper.

2. Make the mixture into 1½-inch balls and lay them on a baking pan sprayed with cooking spray. Arrange them in the Air Fryer.

3. Cook at 370°F for up to 25 minutes. You may now prepare the sauce by mixing together all the ingredients for the sauce in a small mixing bowl.

4. Cook the sauce as you desire. Top with green onions. Serve and enjoy!!!

AIR FRYER POULTRY RECIPES

Chicken Parmesan

Preparation Time: 5 minutes

Cooking Time: 10 minutes

Total Time: 15 minutes

Servings: 4

Calories: 251 kcal

Ingredients:

- 6 Tbsp. seasoned breadcrumbs
- 2 Tbsp. grated Parmesan cheese
- 2 (8 Oz.) Chicken breast, cut in half
- 1 Tbsp. butter, melted
- 6 Tbsp. mozzarella cheese
- ½ Cup of marinara
- Cooking spray

Cooking Instructions:

1. Begin by Preheating the Air Fryer to 360°F. In a small mixing bowl, merge together the breadcrumbs and parmesan cheese.

2. Rub the butter on the chicken and dredge the chicken on the breadcrumb mixture. Arrange 2 pieces in the Air Fryer basket and sprinkle oil on the top.

3. Bake for up to 6 minutes. Flip over and top each with 2 Tbsp. sauce and 1 ½ Tbsp. of shredded mozzarella cheese.

4. Bake for another 3 minutes. Do for the remaining pieces.

5. Serve and enjoy!!!

20 Minute Chicken Breast

Preparation Time: 15 minutes

Cooking Time: 10 minutes

Total Time: 25 minutes

Servings: 4

Calories: 188 kcal

Ingredients:

- 1 Lb. boneless skinless chicken breasts, horizontally cut into half
- 1 Tbsp. olive oil
- Breading:
- ½ Tsp. salt
- ¼ Tsp. black pepper
- ¼ Cup of bread crumbs
- ½ Tsp. paprika
- ⅛ Tsp. garlic powder
- ⅛ Tsp. onion powder
- ⅛ Tsp. cayenne pepper

Cooking Instructions:

1. Begin by Preheating the Air Fryer to 390°F. Rub olive oil on the sides of the chicken breast.

2. Combine together all the breading ingredients. Coat the chicken breast with this mixture.

3. Arrange them in the Air Fryer in batches if need be. Bake for up to 4 minutes, turn over and bake for another 2 minutes.

4. Serve and enjoy!!!

Baked Chicken Drumsticks

Preparation Time: 3 minutes

Cooking Time: 35 minutes

Total Time: 38 minutes

Servings: 6

Calories: 292 kcal

Ingredients:

- 2 Tsp. avocado oil
- 1 Tsp. salt
- 6 Chicken legs raw, with skin
- ¼ Tsp. black pepper
- 1 Tsp. granulated garlic
- ¼ Tsp. paprika
- ¼ Tsp. onion powder

Cooking Instructions:

1. Begin by Preheating the Air Fryer to 400°F. In a small mixing bowl, combine together the salt, pepper, granulated garlic, paprika and onion powder.

2. Using paper towel, blot the drumsticks and lay the on-baking sheet lined with parchment paper. Sprinkle olive oil on the sticks.

3. Pour the seasoning mixture on the chicken legs; turn them over and repeat the same thing on the other side.

4. Bake for 20 minutes. Use tongs and turn the sticks over to the other side and bake for another 15 minutes.

5. Serve and enjoy!!!

Southern Fried Chicken without Buttermilk

Preparation Time: 10 minutes

Cooking Time: 15 minutes

Total Time: 25 minutes

Servings: 8

Calories: 218 kcal

Ingredients:

- 1 Cup of all-purpose flour
- 1 Whole chicken, cut
- 1 Tbsp. salt
- ½ Tsp. pepper
- 2 Eggs
- Oil

Cooking Instructions:

1. Begin by Preheating the Air Fryer to 360°F. Combine together the flour, salt, and pepper. Beat the eggs into another bowl.

2. Take a piece and dredge it in the flour. Shake and burry it in the egg. Repeat with the rest of the pieces.

3. Sprinkle oil on the Air Fryer cooking pan. Place the chicken on the cooking pan and lay it in the Air Fryer. Cook both sides for 8 minutes respectively.

4. Serve and enjoy!!!

Greek Chicken Wraps

Preparation Time: 14 minutes

Cooking Time: 15 minutes

Total Time: 29 minutes

Servings: 4

Calories: 356 kcal

Ingredients:

- 2 Tsp. oregano
- 2 Tsp. basil
- 2 Chicken breasts, chopped
- 2 Small zucchinis, chopped
- 2 Bell peppers, chopped
- 1 Red onion, sliced
- 2 Tbsp. olive oil
- ½ Tsp. garlic powder
- ½ Tsp. onion powder
- ½ Tsp. salt
- 2 Lemons sliced
- ¼ Cup of feta cheese crumbled
- 4 Large flour tortillas or wraps

Cooking Instructions:

1. Begin by Preheating the Air Fryer to 400°F.

2. In a small mixing bowl, mix together the chicken, zucchinis, bell peppers, onion, olive oil, oregano, basil, garlic powder, onion powder and salt.

3. Arrange the lemon slices on a baking sheet. Bake in the Air Fryer for 15 minutes. Share the chicken mixture into a medium container. Top with feta cheese.

4. Serve and enjoy!!!

Chicken Nuggets

Preparation Time: 10 minutes

Cooking Time: 8 minutes

Total Time: 18 minutes

Servings: 4

Calories: 188 kcal

Ingredients:

- Black pepper
- 2 Tsp. olive oil
- 2. (16 Oz.) Large skinless boneless chicken breasts, cut into 1-inch pieces
- ½ Tsp. kosher salt
- 6 Tbsp. whole wheat Italian seasoned breadcrumbs
- 2 Tbsp. panko
- 2 Tbsp. grated parmesan cheese
- Olive oil spray

Cooking Instructions:

1. Begin by Preheating the Air Fryer to 400°F. In a small mixing bowl, combine together the olive oil and breadcrumbs.

2. Mix panko and parmesan cheese in another. Apply salt and pepper on the chicken and burry it in the olive oil bowl. Coat the chicken well in the mixture.

3. Dip few chunks of chicken into the breadcrumb mixture and lay them in the Air fryer cooking basket.

4. Sprinkle with oil and cook for 8 minutes turning halfway through cooking time.

5. Serve and enjoy!!!

Chicken Wings

Preparation Time: 10 minutes

Cooking Time: 30 minutes

Total Time: 40 minutes

Servings: 5

Calories: 266 kcal

Ingredients:

- 1 Tsp. kosher salt
- 1 ½ Lb. chicken wings, flats and drumettes separated, rinsed and pat dry
- 1 Tsp. garlic powder
- ½ Tsp. cayenne pepper

Cooking Instructions:

1. Begin by Preheating the Air Fryer to 400°F. Evenly sprinkle the chicken with salt, garlic powder, and cayenne.

2. Lay the wings in the Air Fryer and cook at 380°F for 25 minutes shaking the basket every 5 minutes.

3. Increase the heat to 400°F and cook for another 5 minutes.

4. Serve and enjoy!!!

Fried Chicken

Preparation Time: 10 minutes

Cooking Time: 20 minutes

Total Time: 30 minutes

Servings: 6

Calories: 318 kcal

Ingredients:

- 1 Tbsp. garlic powder
- 2 Tbsp. paprika
- 1 whole chicken, cut into 10 pieces
- 1 Tbsp. kosher salt, divided
- 1 Tsp. freshly ground black pepper, divided
- 2 Cups of buttermilk
- 2 Cups of all-purpose flour
- 1 Tsp. cayenne pepper
- 1 Tbsp. onion powder
- 1 Tbsp. ground mustard
- Cooking spray

Cooking Instructions:

1. Begin by Preheating the Air Fryer to 400°F. Put the chicken in a large mixing bowl, add salt, pepper, butter milk and allow it to marinate for at least an hour in refrigerator.

2. In a large mixing bowl, mix together the remaining pepper, salt, flour, garlic powder, paprika, cayenne pepper, onion powder and ground mustard.

3. Sprinkle cooking spray on the Air Fryer racks. Remove the chicken from the buttermilk and dip in the flour mixture.

4. Arrange the chicken in the Air Fryer cooking basket and cook for 20 minutes turning the chicken to the other side halfway through the cooking time.

5. Serve and enjoy!!!

Turkey Breast

Preparation Time: 5 minutes

Cooking Time: 20 minutes

Total Time: 25 minutes

Servings: 10

Calories: 226 kcal

Ingredients:

- 4 Lbs. turkey breast, on the bone with skin
- 1 Tbsp. olive oil
- 2 Tsp. kosher
- ½ Tbsp. dry poultry seasoning

Cooking Instructions:

1. Begin by Preheating the Air Fryer to 350°F. Brush half Tsp. on the turkey breast and apply salt and turkey seasoning.

2. Brush the remaining half of oil on the turkey skin side. Place the turkey in the Air Fryer skin side down and cook for 20 minutes.

3. Turn over to the other side and cook again for another 20 minutes.

4. Serve and enjoy!!!

Lemon Pepper Air Fryer Chicken Thighs

Preparation Time: 10 minutes

Cooking Time: 15 minutes

Total Time: 25 minutes

Servings: 6

Calories: 251 kcal

Ingredients:

- 1 ½ Tbsp. fresh lemon juice
- ½ Tbsp. Lemon Pepper Seasoning
- 6 Boneless skinless chicken thighs, washed and dried
- ½ Tsp. Paprika
- ½ Tsp. Italian Seasoning
- ½ Tsp. Garlic Powder
- ¼ Tsp. Black Pepper

Cooking Instructions:

1. Begin by Preheating the Air Fryer to 350°F. Apply all the ingredients over the chicken thighs.

2. Arrange in the Air Fryer and bake at 360°F for up to 15 minutes shaking the basket halfway through the cooking time.

3. Serve and enjoy!!!

Pesto Chicken Pita

Preparation Time: 10 minutes

Cooking Time: 15 minutes

Total Time: 25 minutes

Servings: 4

Calories: 449 kcal

Ingredients:

- 1 Zucchini, cut into tiny pieces
- 2 Tbsp. olive oil
- 1 Lb. boneless skinless chicken breasts, cut into small pieces
- ½ Red onion, sliced
- 2 Bell peppers, chopped
- Salt
- Pepper
- ⅓ Cup pesto
- 4 pita pockets

Cooking Instructions:

1. Begin by Preheating the Air Fryer to 400°F. Apply olive oil on the chicken and also add salt and pepper. Place them on a baking sheet.

2. Place in the Air Fryer at 390°F for 10 minutes. Shake and turn over then cook for another 5 minutes.

3. Put them in a large bowl with pesto and scoop into pita halves.

4. Serve and enjoy!!!

AIR FRYER FISH & SEAFOOD RECIPES

Fish Sticks

Preparation Time: 10 minutes

Cooking Time: 36 minutes

Total Time: 46 minutes

Servings: 4

Calories: 449 kcal

Ingredients:

- ¼ Cup of kraft Grated Parmesan Cheese
- 2 Large Eggs
- ¼ Cup of miracle whip Dressing
- 1 Cup of Italian-seasoned panko bread crumbs
- 1 Lb. cod fillets, cut into smaller pieces

Cooking Instructions:

1. Begin by Preheating the Air Fryer to 390°F. Mix together dressing and eggs in pie plate and stir it thoroughly.

2. Pulse breadcrumbs and cheese in a food processor. Blend it well and pour into pie plate.

3. Dump in fish fillet into egg mixture, remove and fully dip into the breadcrumb mixture.

4. Spray cooking spray on the Air Fryer basket. Arrange the fish in the basket and cook for 12 minutes. Flip onto serving plate.

5. Serve and enjoy!!!

Easy Salmon

Preparation Time: 5 minutes

Cooking Time: 12 minutes

Total Time: 17 minutes

Servings: 4

Calories: 210 kcal

Ingredients:

- 1 Fresh lemon
- 1 Tbsp. olive oil
- 1 Lb. salmon, sliced into fillets, pat dry with paper towel
- 2 Tsp. Primal Palate seafood seasoning
- 2 Tsp. lemon pepper seasoning
- 1 Tsp. garlic powder
- Salt

Cooking Instructions:

1. Begin by Preheating the Air Fryer to 390°F. Put 1 Tbsp. oil into a bowl, put juice of half lemon, mix well and rub the mixture on the salmon.

2. Apply spices and salt on the salmon. Line parchment paper on the Air Fryer basket and lay the salmon on the parchment paper.

3. Cook at 360°F for up 12 minutes. Keep it to cool and then garnish with lemon slices.

4. Serve and enjoy!!!

Salmon Bok Choy

Preparation Time: 20 minutes

Cooking Time: 12 minutes

Total Time: 32 minutes

Servings: 2

Calories: 195 kcal

Ingredients:

- 2 Garlic Cloves, minced
- 1 Tbsp, Minced Ginger
- 2 Tsp. finely grated orange zest
- ½ Cup of fresh orange juice
- ½ Cup of soy Sauce
- 3 Tbsp. Rice Vinegar
- 1 Tbsp. Vegetable Oil
- ½ Tsp. Salt
- 2 5 Oz. Salmon fillets
- For the Vegetables:
- 2 Heads baby bok choy, halved length wise
- 2 Oz. shiitake mushrooms, stem removed
- 1 Tbsp. Dark Sesame Oil
- Salt
- ½ Tsp. Sesame Seeds, toasted

Cooking Instructions:

1. Begin by Preheating the Air Fryer to 400°F. In a small mixing bowl, merge together the garlic, ginger, orange zest and juice.

2. Add the soy sauce, vinegar, vegetable oil, and salt. Remove half of the marinade and set aside.

3. Put the salmon on a gallon-size resealable bag. Put the reserved half of marinade on top of the salmon.

4. Tight the bag and give a good massage to coat. Set aside for about 30 minutes. Lay the bag in the Air Fryer basket and cook at 400°F for about 12 minutes.

5. Rub sea same oil on bok choy and mushroom caps and apply salt. When it is half time to the cooking time, add vegetables around salmon in Air Fryer basket.

6. Continue cooking for remaining 6 minutes. Sprinkle the salmon with some of the reserved marinade and top the vegetables with sesame seeds.

7. Serve and enjoy!!!

Spicy Crab Dip

Preparation Time: 5 minutes

Cooking Time: 7 minutes

Total Time: 12 minutes

Servings: 4

Calories: 359 kcal

Ingredients:

- ½ Cup of Green Onions
- 2 Tbsp. Louisiana Hot Sauce
- 1 Cup of cooked crab
- ¼ Cup of mayonnaise
- 2 Cups of grated jalapeno jack cheese
- ½ Tsp. Salt
- 1 Tsp. Ground Black Pepper
- 2 Tbsp. lemon juice
- 2 Tbsp. Chopped Parsley

Cooking Instructions:

1. Begin by Preheating the Air Fryer to 400°F. Merge together the crab, mayonnaise, cheese, scallions hot sauce salt and pepper in a baking pan.

2. Lay the pan in the Air Fryer cooking basket and cook at 400°F for 7 minutes. Get the pan out and pour lemon juice and parsley.

3. Serve and enjoy!!!

Gorton's Fish Fillets

Preparation Time: 5 minutes

Cooking Time: 9 minutes

Total Time: 14 minutes

Servings: 2

Calories: 182 kcal

Ingredients:

- 2 Fish Fillets
- Oil

Cooking Instructions:

1. Begin by Preheating the Air Fryer to 390°F Sprinkle oil all over the fish fillets.

2. Place them in the Air Fryer cooking basket and cook for 9 minutes shaking halfway to the cooking time.

3. Serve and enjoy!!!

Salt and Pepper Shrimp

Preparation Time: 10 minutes

Cooking Time: 10 minutes

Total Time: 20 minutes

Servings: 4

Calories: 178 kcal

Ingredients:

- 2 Tsp. Sichuan peppercorns, ground
- 1 Tsp. Salt
- 2 Tsp. Whole Black Peppercorns, ground
- 1 Tsp. Sugar
- 1 Lb. Shrimp
- 3 Tbsp. Rice Flour
- 2 Tbsp. Oil

Cooking Instructions:

1. Begin by Preheating the Air Fryer to 390°F. In a saucepan, heat up and roast the black peppercorns and Sichuan peppercorns together for 2 minutes.

2. Allow it to cool. Put salt and sugar, and use a mortar and pestle to crush the spices in order to make a coarse powder.

3. Lay shrimp in a large mixing bowl and put the spices, rice flour and oil. Stir thoroughly. Arrange the shrimp in the Air Fryer cooking basket.

4. Spray additional oil and cook the shrimp at 325°F for up to 10 minutes. When it is halfway through the cooking time, turn the basket.

5. Serve and enjoy!!!

Spicy Garlic Prawn

Preparation Time: 12 minutes

Cooking Time: 8 minutes

Total Time: 20 minutes

Servings: 3

Calories: 219 kcal

Ingredients:

- 1 ½ Tbsp. Olive Oil
- 1 Tsp. Chilli Powder
- 15 Fresh Prawns, washed and rinsed
- 1 Tsp. Black Pepper
- 1 Tbsp. Sweet Chilli Sauce
- 1 Garlic, minced
- Salt

Cooking Instructions:

1. Begin by Preheating the Air Fryer to 390°F. In a small mixing bowl, merge together the prawns, oil, chilli powder, pepper, salt, chilli sauce and garlic.

2. Give it a thorough mix. Lay the prawns in the Air Fryer cooking basket and cook at 390°F for 8 minutes.

3. Serve and enjoy!!!

King Prawns

Preparation Time: 5 minutes

Cooking Time: 8 minutes

Total Time: 13 minutes

Servings: 2

Calories: 317 kcal

Ingredients:

- ½ Onion, chopped
- 2 Garlic cloves, chopped
- 400g king prawns peeled, uncooked
- 2 Tbsp. olive oil
- ½ Lemon
- 1 pinch sea salt
- Black pepper
- Parsley, chopped

Cooking Instructions:

1. Begin by Preheating the Air Fryer to 370°F. In a small mixing bowl, merge together the prawns, onions, garlic and parsley. Stir well and set aside.

2. Place the mixture in a baking pan and lay it in the Air Fryer cooking basket. Cook at 400°F for 8 minutes. Garnish with lemon wedges.

3. Serve and enjoy!!!

White Fish with Garlic and Lemon

Preparation Time: 5 minutes

Cooking Time: 10 minutes

Total Time: 15 minutes

Servings: 2

Calories: 169 kcal

Ingredients:

- ½ Tsp. garlic powder
- ½ Tsp. lemon pepper seasoning
- 12 Oz. tilapia filets, rinsed and pat dried
- Kosher salt
- Fresh cracked black pepper
- Fresh chopped parsley
- Lemon wedges

Cooking Instructions:

1. Begin by Preheating the Air Fryer to 360°F. Spray the fillets with olive oil on both sides. Add garlic powder, lemon pepper, salt and pepper.

2. Line parchment paper in the Air Fryer cooking basket and spray small oil. Arrange the fillets on the paper and pour some lemon wedges.

3. Cook at 360°F for about 10 minutes and sprinkle with chopped parsley and top with the toasted lemon wedges.

4. Serve and enjoy!!!

Garlic Parmesan Air Fried Shrimp

Preparation Time: 10 minutes

Cooking Time: 10 minutes

Total Time: 20 minutes

Servings: 2

Calories: 228 kcal

Ingredients:

- 1 Tbsp. olive oil
- 1 Tsp. salt
- 1 Lb. shrimp, deveined and peeled
- 1 Tsp. fresh cracked pepper
- 1 Tbsp. lemon juice
- 6 Cloves garlic, diced
- ½ Cup of grated parmesan cheese

Cooking Instructions:

1. Begin by Preheating the Air Fryer to 360°F. Merge together the shrimp, olive oil, lemon juice, salt, pepper, and garlic in a large mixing bowl.

2. Close and put in the refrigerator for 3 hours. Dredge the parmesan cheese into bowl with shrimp, creating a kind of breading for the shrimp.

3. Place the shrimp in the Air Fryer cooking basket and cook at 350°F for 10 minutes.

4. Serve and enjoy!!!

Shrimp Fried Rice

Preparation Time: 10 minutes

Cooking Time: 25 minutes

Total Time: 35 minutes

Servings: 4

Calories: 344 kcal

Ingredients:

For the Shrimp:

- 1 Lb. Shrimp, peeled and deveined
- ¼ Tsp. pepper
- 1 Tsp. Cornstarch
- For the Rice:
- 2 Cups of cooked rice
- 1 Cup of frozen peas and carrots, thawed
- ¼ Cup of green onions, chopped
- 3 Tbsp. sesame oil
- 1 Tbsp. soy sauce
- ½ Tsp. salt
- 1 Tsp. pepper

For the Eggs:

- 2 Large Eggs, beaten
- ¼ Tsp. salt
- ¼ Tsp. pepper

Cooking Instructions:

1. Begin by Preheating the Air Fryer to 360°F. Merge together the shrimp, salt and cornstarch and keep aside.

2. Combine together the rice, vegetables, onions, sesame oil, salt, and pepper. Place in the Air Fryer.

3. Cook at 350°F for 15 minutes shaking the rice halfway through cook time. Lay the shrimp on the rice.

4. Cook for another 5 minutes using the same heat. Beat the eggs and mix with salt and pepper.

5. Pour the eggs mixture on top of the shrimp and rice mixture and cook for another 5 minutes using the same heat. Turn the eggs into the shrimp and rice.

6. Serve and enjoy!!!

Shrimp Scampi

Preparation Time: 5 minutes

Cooking Time: 10 minutes

Total Time: 15 minutes

Servings: 4

Calories: 188 kcal

Ingredients:

- 1 Tbsp. Minced Garlic
- 1 Tsp. Smoked Paprika
- 4 Tbsp. Butter
- 1 Tsp. dried basil
- 2 Tbsp. Chicken Stock
- 1 Lb. Shrimp, defrosted
- 1 Tbsp. lemon juice

Cooking Instructions:

1. Begin by Preheating the Air Fryer to 400°F. In a small mixing bowl, merge together the butter, garlic, smoked paprika and basil and set aside.

2. Add shrimp and chicken stock and stir thoroughly coating the shrimp with the sauce.

3. Place the mixture in the Air Fryer and cook for 10 minutes. Add lemon juice.

4. Serve and enjoy!!!

AIR FRYER BEEF & PORK RECIPES

Kenyan Braised Collard Greens and Ground Beef

Preparation Time: 15 minutes

Cooking Time: 15 minutes

Total Time: 30 minutes

Servings: 4

Calories: 263 kcal

Ingredients:

- ½ Tsp. turmeric
- 1 Tsp. kosher salt
- 1 Tsp. ground cumin
- 1 Tsp. olive oil
- ½ White onion, chopped
- 2 Cloves garlic, chopped
- 1 Jalapeno, seeded and chopped
- 1 Lb. ground beef
- ½ Tsp. black pepper
- ½ Tsp. ground cinnamon
- ⅓ Tsp. ground ginger
- 1 Tsp. ground coriander
- 1 Bunch, 8 leaves collard greens, stems removed sliced into srips
- 15 Grape tomatoes, quartered
- 1 Tsp. lemon juice

Cooking Instructions:

1. Begin by Preheating the Air Fryer to 400°F. Merge together onions, garlic, jalapeno, ground beef, Seasonings, collard greens and tomatoes. Stir well.

2. Put lemon juice, salt and pepper. Stir well and place in the Air Fryer basket and then cook for 15 minutes shaking halfway through the cooking time.

3. Serve and enjoy!!!

Italian Beef Hoagies

Preparation Time: 15 minutes

Cooking Time: 6 hours 5 minutes

Total Time: 6 hours 20 minutes

Servings: 8

Calories: 442 kcal

Ingredients:

- 1 Tbsp. minced garlic
- 1 Bay leaf
- 3 Lbs. beef top round roast, fat trimmed out and pat dry with paper towel
- ½ Tsp. onion powder
- ½ Tsp. black pepper
- ½ Tsp. salt
- 4 Tsp. Italian salad dressing mix
- 3 Cups of beef broth
- 16 Oz. jar pepperoncini
- 2 Red bell peppers, cut into thin strips
- 8 2 Oz. pieces whole wheat Italian bread
- 8 Slices Sargento Provolone Ultra Thin
- For Homemade Italian Seasoning:
- 1 ½ Tbsp. garlic powder
- 1½ Tbsp. onion powder
- 1 Tbsp. sugar
- 2 Tbsp. dried parsley
- 1 Tbsp. dried oregano
- ½ Tsp. dried thyme
- 1 Tsp. dried basil
- 1 Tbsp. salt
- 2 Tsp. black pepper

Cooking Instructions:

1. Begin by Preheating the Air Fryer to 400°F. In a small mixing bowl, merge together the onion powder, black pepper and salt.

2. Mix well and rub the mixture all over the roast then put in the Air Fryer cooking basket.

3. Put the Italian salad dressing mix, broth, garlic, pepperoncinis, bell peppers and bay leaf. Cook in the Air Fryer at 400°F for 6 hours 30 minutes.

4. When it is done, remove bay leaf and shred the beef. Top each of the bread with 3 Oz. meat mixture and 1 slice cheese.

5. Serve and enjoy!!!

Bacon Burger Bites

Preparation Time: 10 minutes

Cooking Time: 20 minutes

Total Time: 30 minutes

Servings: 15

Calories: 125 kcal

Ingredients:

- ⅓ Tsp. kosher salt
- ½ Tsp. onion powder
- 2 Lbs. beef
- 4 Oz. center cut raw bacon, minced
- 2 Tbsp. yellow mustard
- ¼ Tsp. black pepper
- 1 Head butter lettuce
- 30 Cherry tomatoes
- 30 Dill pickle chips

Cooking Instructions:

1. Begin by Preheating the Air Fryer to 400°F. In a small mixing bowl, merge together the beef, bacon, mustard, salt, onion powder and pepper.

2. Form about 30 ball shapes. Arrange the balls in the Air Fryer cooking basket and bake at 390°F for 10 minutes turning halfway to the cooking time.

3. Lay each burger on a skewer with lettuce, pickles and tomatoes.

4. Serve and enjoy!!!

Beef Empanadas

Preparation Time: 10 minutes

Cooking Time: 16 minutes

Total Time: 26 minutes

Servings: 8

Calories: 183 kcal

Ingredients:

- 1 Cup of picadillo
- 8 Goya empanada discs, in frozen section, thawed
- 1 Egg white, whisked
- 1 Tsp. water

Cooking Instructions:

1. Begin by Preheating the Air Fryer to 325°F. Spray cooking spray on the Air Fryer cooking basket.

2. Lay 2 Tbsp. of picadillo in the center of each disc. Fold in half closing the edges with fork. Do this for all the doughs.

3. Merge together water and egg whites, and then brush the tops of the empanadas with the mixture.

4. Place in the Air Fryer basket and cook in batches for up to 8 minutes.

5. Serve and enjoy!!!

Beef Jerky

Preparation Time: 10 minutes

Cooking Time: 3 hours

Total Time: 3 hours 10 minutes

Servings: 8

Calories: 69 kcal

Ingredients:

- 1 Garlic clove, minced
- 1 Inch Piece of fresh gingerroot, peeled and grated
- 12 Oz. top sirloin beef
- 2 Tbsp. soy sauce
- 1 Tbsp. turbinado sugar
- 1 Tbsp. chili paste
- 1 Tbsp. rice vinegar

Cooking Instructions:

1. Begin by Preheating the Air Fryer to 325°F. Slice beef and put on a bag that can be sealed.

2. Merge together garlic, ginger, soy sauce, sugar chili paste and rice vinegar. Give it a good stir. Put the mixture into the bag and tight it.

3. Put in the refrigerator for 8 hours. When you are ready to cook, remove some pieces of beef from a marinade and pat dry using a paper towel.

4. Arrange the beef in the Air Fryer basket and cook for up to 3 hours. While cooking you have to regularly check for proper doneness.

5. Remove it and allow it to cool completely.

6. Serve and enjoy!!!

Pork Chops

Preparation Time: 2 minutes

Cooking Time: 12 minutes

Total Time: 14 minutes

Servings: 1

Calories: 214 kcal

Ingredients:

- 1 pork chop, pat dried
- ½ Tsp. seasoning

Cooking Instructions:

1. Begin by Preheating the Air Fryer to 360°F. Apply salt and pepper on the pork chop.

2. Arrange the pork in the Air Fryer cooking basket. Do not allow them to overlap. Cook for up to 12 minutes.

3. Serve and enjoy!!!

Roast Lamb

Preparation Time: 5 minutes

Cooking Time: 15 minutes

Total Time: 20 minutes

Servings: 2

Calories: 181 kcal

Ingredients:

- 10 Oz. butterflies lamb leg roast, pat dried
- 1 Tbsp. olive oil
- 1 Tsp. rosemary fresh
- 1 Tsp. thyme fresh
- ½ Tsp. black pepper

Cooking Instructions:

1. Begin by Preheating the Air Fryer to 360°F. Combine together the olive oil, rosemary and thyme in a small mixing bowl.

2. Put the lamb roast in the oil mixture and stir it well. Arrange the lamb in the Air Fryer basket. Cook for up to 15 minutes.

3. Remove roast lamb from air fryer, close with kitchen foil and keep it for 5 minutes.

4. Serve and enjoy!!!

Roast Pork

Preparation Time: 10 minutes

Cooking Time: 50 minutes

Total Time: 60 minutes

Servings: 7

Calories: 220 kcal

Ingredients:

- 2 Lb. pork loin
- 1 Tbsp. olive oil
- 1 Tsp. salt

Cooking Instructions:

1. Begin by Preheating the Air Fryer to 360°F. Sprinkle oil on the pork and make it to touch the skin and season with salt all over the skin.

2. Place the pork in the Air Fryer basket and cook for 50 minutes. Remove from the Air Fryer, close with aluminum foil and set aside for 10 minutes.

3. Serve and enjoy!!!

Garlic Lovers Roast Beef

Preparation Time: 5 minutes

Cooking Time: 1 hour 15 minutes

Total Time: 1 hour 20 minutes

Servings: 10

Calories: 143 kcal

Ingredients:

- Olive oil spray
- Kosher salt
- 3 Lb. roast or eye round, all fat trimmed off
- 3 Cloves garlic, sliced
- Fresh cracked pepper
- 2 Tsp. dried chopped rosemary

Cooking Instructions:

1. Begin by Preheating the Air Fryer to 360°F. Use sharp knife and Pierce the meat deep and put sliced garlic in each of the hole.

2. Pour small olive oil on the meat and apply rosemary, salt and pepper to your taste. Put the meat in the cooking pan.

3. Place the pan in the Air Fryer basket and cook for about 20 minutes. Remove from heat and slice it.

4. Serve and enjoy!!!

Cajun Pork Burgers

Preparation Time: 20 minutes

Cooking Time: 10 minutes

Total Time: 30 minutes

Servings: 2

Calories: 704 kcal

Ingredients:

- Pork burger patties
- ½ Lb. pork mince
- 1 Tbsp. Cajun seasoning
- ½ Cup of fine breadcrumbs
- 1 Egg
- Salt
- Pepper
- Olive oil
- Burger bun and toppings:
- 2 burger buns
- 1 tomato sliced
- ½ avocado sliced

Cooking Instructions:

1. Begin by Preheating the Air Fryer to 370°F. In a small mixing bowl merge together the pork mince, Cajun seasoning, breadcrumbs egg, salt and pepper.

2. Make the prepared mixture into Patty sizes. Grease the Air Fryer basket with oil and arrange the patties in the Air Fryer basket separating each other.

3. Cook for about 10 minutes. When they are not yet done, cut the burger buns into 2 and put under a hot broiler for about 2 minutes.

4. Top with tomato and avocado slices.

5. Serve and enjoy!!!

AIR FRYER MAIN MEAL RECIPES

Lemon Pepper Chicken

Preparation Time: 3 minutes

Cooking Time: 15 minutes

Total Time: 18 minutes

Servings: 3

Calories: 140 kcal

Ingredients:

- 2 Lemons rind and juice
- 1 Tbsp. Chicken Seasoning
- Whole30 Book
- 1 Chicken Breast
- 1 Tsp. Garlic Puree
- Handful Black Peppercorns
- Salt
- Pepper

Cooking Instructions:

1. Begin by Preheating the Air Fryer to 360°F. Put a large sheet of silver foil on the work top and put all the seasonings and the lemon rind.

2. Place your chicken breast a cutting board and cut out any fat or any bone. Apply salt and pepper. Apply the chicken seasoning in both sides.

3. Use rolling pin and give it a slap to enable it flattened. Put it in the Air Fryer and cook for 15 minutes.

4. Serve and enjoy!!!

Thai Salmon Patties

Preparation Time: 15 minutes

Cooking Time: 8 minutes

Total Time: 23 minutes

Servings: 7

Calories: 108 kcal

Ingredients:

- ¼ Tsp. salt
- 1 ½ Tbsp. Thai red curry paste
- 14 Oz. canned salmon drained
- ½ Cup of Panko breadcrumbs
- 1 ½ Tbsp. brown sugar
- Zest from 1 lime
- 2 Eggs
- Spray oil

Cooking Instructions:

1. Begin by Preheating the Air Fryer to 360°F. In a small mixing bowl merge together all the ingredients and mix well. Shape into patties of your sizes.

2. Spray oil all over the patties and arrange them in the Air Fryer and cook for 8 minutes turning halfway through the cooking time. Flip onto a serving plate.

3. Serve and enjoy!!!

Fish Finger Sandwich

Preparation Time: 5 minutes

Cooking Time: 15 minutes

Total Time: 20 minutes

Servings: 4

Calories: 281 kcal

Ingredients:

- Spray oil
- 250g Frozen peas
- 4 Small cod fillets, skin removed
- Salt
- Pepper
- 2 Tbsp. flour
- 40g Dried breadcrumbs
- 1 Tbsp. creme fraiche
- 12 Capers
- Squeeze of lemon juice
- 4 Bread rolls

Cooking Instructions:

1. Begin by Preheating the Air Fryer to 360°F. Apply salt and pepper on the cod fillets and roll in the flour and breadcrumbs respectively.

2. Spray the Air Fryer basket with oil. Arrange the cod fillets on the Air Fryer basket and cook for about 15 minutes.

3. When the fish is yet to be fully cooked, cook the peas in a boiling water using microwave. Remove and put into a food processor.

4. Put creme fraiches, capers and lemon juice and blend properly. When the fish is completely cooked, remove it from heat.

5. Place the sandwich with the bread, fish and pea puree. Serve and enjoy!

Hot Dog

Preparation Time: 3 minutes

Cooking Time: 7 minutes

Total Time: 10 minutes

Servings: 2

Calories: 289 kcal

Ingredients:

- 2 Hot dogs
- 2 Hot dog buns
- 2 Tbsp. grated cheese

Cooking Instructions:

1. Begin by Preheating the Air Fryer to 390°F. Arrange 2 hot dogs in the Air Fryer basket and cook for at least 5 minutes.

2. Get the hot dog out from the Air Fryer and put it on a bun. Put cheese. Put the hot dog again in the Air Fryer and cook for another 2 minutes.

3. Serve and enjoy!!!

Tandoori Paneer Naan Pizza

Preparation Time: 10 minutes

Cooking Time: 10 minutes

Total Time: 20 minutes

Servings: 2

Calories: 738 kcal

Ingredients:

- ¼ Cup of Pizza sauce
- ¼ Cup of Grape Tomatoes, halved
- 2 Garlic Naan
- ¼ Cup of Red Onions sliced
- ⅛ Cup of Bell pepper sliced
- ¾ Cup of Mozzarella grated
- 2 Tbsp. Cilantro chopped
- For Tandoori Paneer:
- ½ Tsp. Garam Masala
- ½ Tsp. Garlic powder
- ½ Cup of Paneer small cubes
- 1 Tbsp. Yogurt thick
- ¼ Tsp. Ground Turmeric
- ⅓ Tsp. Kashmiri Red Chili powder
- ¼ Tsp. Salt

Cooking Instructions:

1. Begin by Preheating the Air Fryer to 390°F. For the Tandoori Paneer, combine all the ingredients in a small mixing bowl and stir well.

2. Place parchment paper on a baking tray. Put naans on the tray and evenly put sauce on it and small mozzarella.

3. Lay the paneer cubes and spread red onions, bell peppers and grape tomatoes. Equally pour mozzarella on the top of veggies and top with chopped Cilantro.

4. Cook in the Air Fryer for 10 minutes turning halfway to cooking time. Top with chili flake. Serve and enjoy!!!

Meatball Parmesan Casserole

Preparation Time: 10 minutes

Cooking Time: 35 minutes

Total Time: 45 minutes

Servings: 4

Calories: 182 kcal

Ingredients:

- 20 Cooked Perfect meatballs
- 1 Jar (24 Oz.) Spaghetti sauce
- ½ Cup of parmesan cheese, shredded
- 1 Cup of mozzarella cheese, shredded

Cooking Instructions:

1. Begin by Preheating the Air Fryer to 390°F. Put half of the spaghetti sauce into a baking pan. Place meatballs on the top.

2. Spread the remaining sauce on the meatballs. Place shredded parmesan and mozzarella on the top.

3. Place them in the Air Fryer cooking basket and cook for about 35 minutes. Check that it is fully cooked.

4. Serve and enjoy!!!

Air Fryer Tofu

Preparation Time: 10 minutes

Cooking Time: 13 minutes

Total Time: 23 minutes

Servings: 4

Calories: 94 kcal

Ingredients:

- 2 Tsp. cornstarch
- 1 Tsp. paprika
- 12 Oz. block extra firm tofu, cut into 1/2 inch
- 1 Tbsp. avocado oil
- 1 Tsp. onion powder
- 1 Tsp. garlic powder
- ½ Tsp. black pepper
- ½ Tsp. salt

Cooking Instructions:

1. Begin by Preheating the Air Fryer to 390°F. Toss tofu in avocado oil and cornstarch respectively.

2. Toss tofu again in all the ingredients that remains and lay the tofu in the Air Fryer basket and cook for 13 minutes flipping over every 5 minutes.

3. Serve and enjoy!!!

Sweet Chili Fish Wraps

Preparation Time: 10 minutes

Cooking Time: 15 minutes

Total Time: 25 minutes

Servings: 3

Calories: 195 kcal

Ingredients:

- Gorton's Go Saucy Sweet Chili Tenders
- 2 Large red peppers, sliced
- 2 Avocados, sliced
- 3 Cup of arugula
- 3 Floured tortillas
- Go Saucy Sweet Chili Sauce Packet

Cooking Instructions:

1. Begin by Preheating the Air Fryer to 390°F. In a small mixing bowl merge together the red pepper, avocado, and arugula. Mix well.

2. Put the tenders in the Air Fryer alongside with the above mixture. Cook for about 15 minutes turning halfway to the cooking time.

3. Flip onto a serving plate alongside the tortilla and drizzle with sauce and roll the tortilla up into a wrap.

4. Serve and enjoy!!!

Baked Tofu Steaks with Lemon and Garlic

Preparation Time: 1 hour 15 minutes

Cooking Time: 40 minutes

Total Time: 1 hour 55 minutes

Servings: 4

Calories: 194 kcal

Ingredients:

- 4 Cloves garlic, minced
- 2 Tbsp. lemon zest
- 1 Package tofu (16 Oz.)
- 4 Olive oil
- 4 Tbsp. lemon juice
- 1 Tsp. fresh thyme
- salt
- pepper

Cooking Instructions:

1. Begin by Preheating the Air Fryer to 390°F. Line parchment paper on baking pan. Put the olive oil, and olive oil.

2. Add the garlic, lemon zest, lemon juice, thyme, salt and pepper into the baking pan. Slice the tofu into 8 pieces.

3. Apply the marinade all over the tofu and lay it in the baking pan. Place in the Air Fryer cooking basket and cook for at least 40 minutes.

4. Serve and enjoy!!!

Smoky Bean Chili

Preparation Time: 10 minutes

Cooking Time: 7 minutes

Total Time: 17 minutes

Servings: 4

Calories: 281 kcal

Ingredients:

- 1 Tsp. smoked paprika
- 2 Tsp. chipotle chili paste
- ½ Tbsp. oil
- Frozen onions
- Frozen garlic
- 1 Tsp. ground cumin
- 1 Tin tomatoes
- 1 Tin black beans, drained
- 1 Tin kidney beans, drained
- 100g Frozen peas and corn

Cooking Instructions:

1. Begin by Preheating the Air Fryer to 400°F. Line parchment paper on baking pan.

2. Combine together the oil, onions and garlic, cumin, paprika and chipotle paste and give it a thorough stir.

3. Put the tin tomatoes, black beans and kidney beans and stir well. Add the peas and corn and give it a nice mix.

4. Place in the Air Fryer cooking basket and bake for 7 minutes shaking halfway through the cooking time.

5. Serve and enjoy!!!

AIR FRYER EGG RECIPES

Herb Zucchini and Kale Egg Bake

Preparation Time: 15 minutes

Cooking Time: 30 minutes

Total Time: 45 minutes

Servings: 4

Calories: 302 kcal

Ingredients:

- ½ Tsp. oregano
- ½ Tsp. dill
- 6 Eggs
- ½ Cup of milk
- ½ Cup of almond flour
- ½ Tsp. baking powder
- ¼ Tsp. salt
- ½ Tsp. basil
- 1 Cup of zucchini, shredded and excess moisture squeezed out
- 1 Onion, chopped
- 1 Cup of kale, chopped
- 1 Cup of shredded cheese

Cooking Instructions:

1. Begin by Preheating the Air Fryer to 370°F and spray cooking spray on a baking pan. Merge all the ingredients together in a large mixing bowl and stir well.

2. Put the mixture into the oiled baking pan and place in the Air Fryer basket and cook at 380°F for 30 minutes. Slice it when it is cool.

3. Serve and enjoy!!!

Baked Egg Cups with Spinach and Cheese

Preparation Time: 5 minutes

Cooking Time: 10 minutes

Total Time: 15 minutes

Servings: 1

Calories: 115 kcal

Ingredients:

- 1 Tbsp. milk
- 1 Tbsp. frozen spinach, thawed
- 1 Large egg
- 1 Tsp. grated cheese
- Salt
- Black pepper
- Cooking Spray

Cooking Instructions:

1. Begin by Preheating the Air Fryer to 400°F. Spray cooking spray on the muffin cups.

2. Put egg, milk, salt, pepper, spinach and cheese into the muffin cup. Carefully stir ingredient into egg whites. Do not break the egg yolk.

3. Place in the Air Fryer basket and cook for about 10 minutes shaking halfway through the cooking time.

4. Serve and enjoy!!!

Broccoli Cheese Chicken Egg Rolls

Preparation Time: 10 minutes

Cooking Time: 20 minutes

Total Time: 30 minutes

Servings: 6

Calories: 265 kcal

Ingredients:

- ½ Tsp. Kosher Salt
- Fresh cracked Black Pepper
- 1 Lb. ground Chicken
- 2 Cups of chopped Broccoli floret, chopped
- 3 Large cloves Garlic, minced
- ½ Medium Onion, minced
- 6 Oz. grated Cheese
- 1 Tbsp. Soy Sauce
- 1 Package Egg Roll Wrappers
- 1 Egg, beaten
- Oil
- Hoisin Peanut Dip

Cooking Instructions:

1. Begin by Preheating the Air Fryer to 400°F. Mix together all the ingredients in a large mixing bowl.

2. Give it a nice and thorough stir. Put about 2 Tbsp. of chicken filling into egg roll wrappers.

3. Roll the egg wrapper around the filling, use the beaten egg and brush the top corner of the wrapper.

4. Roll the egg roll completely. Pour oil on the baking pan and place in the Air Fryer basket and cook for 6 minutes turning halfway to cooking time.

5. Serve and enjoy!!!

Quinoa Egg Muffins

Preparation Time: 10 minutes

Cooking Time: 30 minutes

Total Time: 40 minutes

Servings: 12

Calories: 118 kcal

Ingredients:

- ¼ Tsp. pepper
- ¼ Tsp. salt
- 6 Eggs
- 1 Cup of quinoa
- 1 Cup of Swiss cheese
- 1 Cup of mushrooms, chopped
- ½ Cup of sundried tomatoes, drained and chopped

Cooking Instructions:

1. Begin by Preheating the Air Fryer to 350°F. Combine together the eggs, salt and pepper. Put the rest of the ingredients.

2. Scoop into muffin pan lined with parchment muffin liners and put cheese on the top. Place in the Air Fryer and cook for 20 minutes.

3. Serve and enjoy!!!

Cheesy Egg Taco-Dilla

Preparation Time: 2 minutes

Cooking Time: 5 minutes

Total Time: 7 minutes

Servings: 1

Calories: 323 kcal

Ingredients:

- Salt
- Black pepper
- 1 Flour tortilla
- 2 Large eggs, beaten
- 1 Tbsp. butter
- 2 Tbsp. shredded cheese

Cooking Instructions:

1. Begin by Preheating the Air Fryer to 380°F. Put salt and pet in the beaten egg and place the mixture in a baking pan.

2. Put in the Air Fryer basket and air fry for 4 minutes. Halfway to the cooking time, remove the pan, put tortilla on top of the eggs and release the egg from the pan.

3. Turn the egg with the tortilla to the other side and lay on the pan. Put cheese on top of the egg and place back in the Air Fryer basket. Cook for another 4 minutes.

4. Serve and enjoy!!!

Scotch Eggs

Preparation Time: 15 minutes

Cooking Time: 15 minutes

Total Time: 30 minutes

Servings: 6

Calories: 323 kcal

Ingredients:

- 1 Lb. uncooked bulk sausage
- 6 Hardboiled eggs, peeled
- 2 Raw eggs, beaten
- 1 Cup of coating choice
- Hot sauce oil spray

Cooking Instructions:

1. Begin by Preheating the Air Fryer to 380°F. Share the sausage into 5 equal parts. Make each of them into thin patty.

2. Place boiled egg in the middle and fold sausage around the egg. Dump the folded egg into the beaten eggs and dip in breading.

3. Spray oil on the outside of the fully coated egg. Lay in the Air Fryer basket and cook for about 12 minutes turning halfway through cooking time.

4. Serve and enjoy!!!

Bacon And Cheese Egg Muffins

Preparation Time: 15 minutes

Cooking Time: 15 minutes

Total Time: 30 minutes

Servings: 12

Calories: 223 kcal

Ingredients:

- ½ Cup of onion, chopped
- ½ Medium of green pepper, chopped
- 12 Eggs
- Salt
- Pepper
- 6 Slices of Butcher Box bacon, cooked and crumbled
- ½ Medium of red pepper, chopped
- ½ Cup of shredded mozzarella cheese
- ½ Cup of shredded cheddar cheese
- ½ Cup of fresh spinach, chopped

Cooking Instructions:

1. Begin by Preheating the Air Fryer to 350°F. Combine the egg, salt and pepper in a large mixing bowl. Spray olive oil on the muffin tin. Fill the egg halfway into tins.

2. In a small mixing bowl, mix bacon, onions, peppers, and mushrooms, stir and put them into each of the tins. Lay the veggies on the top of the eggs.

3. Put shredded cheese on top and place them in the Air Fryer basket. Cook for 15 minutes. Allow it to cool.

4. Serve and enjoy!!!

Sheet Pan Eggs

Preparation Time: 10 minutes

Cooking Time: 20 minutes

Total Time: 30 minutes

Servings: 12

Calories: 151 kcal

Ingredients:

- ½ Tsp. salt
- ½ Tsp. pepper
- 18 Large eggs, beaten
- ¾ Cup of milk
- 1 Cup of bell peppers, chopped
- 1 Cup of mushrooms, chopped
- ½ Cup of bacon, cooked and chopped
- 1 Cup of shredded cheese

Cooking Instructions:

1. Begin by Preheating the Air Fryer to 375°F. Spray olive oil on a baking pan. In a large mixing bowl, combine together the milk, salt and pepper.

2. Give it a thorough stir. Put the egg mixture into the baking pan. Add bell pepper, mushrooms, bacon and cheese.

3. Arrange the pan in the Air Fryer and bake for 10 minutes. Flip over and cook for another 10 minutes.

4. Serve and enjoy!!!

Baked Eggs

Preparation Time: 10 minutes

Cooking Time: 15 minutes

Total Time: 25 minutes

Servings: 12

Calories: 62 kcal

Ingredients:

- Salt
- 12 Eggs
- Pepper

Cooking Instructions:

1. Begin by Preheating the Air Fryer to 350°F. Pour olive oil on a muffin tin. Beat the eggs into the muffins.

2. Put salt and pepper. Place the muffin in the Air Fryer basket and bake for 15 minutes. Confirm that the eggs are completely done.

3. Serve and enjoy!!!

AIR FRYER SIDE DISH RECIPES

Maple Butter Acorn Squash

Preparation Time: 15 minutes

Cooking Time: 20 minutes

Total Time: 35 minutes

Servings: 4

Calories: 200 kcal

Ingredients:

- ½ Tsp. cinnamon
- 1 Acorn squash, cut, seeded and sliced
- ¼ Cup of salted butter
- ¼ Cup of maple syrup
- Flaky sea salt

Cooking Instructions:

1. Begin by Preheating the Air Fryer to 400°F. Line parchment paper on a baking sheet.

2. In a small mixing bowl, combine together butter, Maple syrup, cinnamon. Mix well. Toss the acorn squash into the mixture and coat well.

3. Lay it on the baking pan and place the pan in the Air Fryer cooking basket and cook for 15 minutes.

4. Remove and brush the squash with more butter and cook for 5 minutes. Season with salt.

5. Serve and enjoy!!!

Maple Cinnamon Roasted Butternut Squash

Preparation Time: 15 minutes

Cooking Time: 30 minutes

Total Time: 45 minutes

Servings: 4

Calories: 130 kcal

Ingredients:

- 1 Tbsp. maple syrup
- ½ Tsp. cinnamon
- 1 Butternut squash, peeled, seeds removed, and sliced into 3/4 inch cubes
- 1 Tbsp. olive oil
- ½ Tsp. paprika
- ½ Tsp. salt

Cooking Instructions:

1. Begin by Preheating the Air Fryer to 400°F. Mix together olive oil, Marple syrup, cinnamon and paprika and toss butternut squash in the mixture and coat well.

2. Oil a baking pan and put the mixture. Place in the Air Fryer basket and cook for 15 minutes. Flip over and cook for another 15 minutes.

3. Serve and enjoy!!!

Coconut Cranberry Muffins

Preparation Time: 15 minutes

Cooking Time: 20 minutes

Total Time: 35 minutes

Servings: 12

Calories: 192 kcal

Ingredients:

- 2 Tsp. baking powder
- 1 Tsp. baking soda
- ¼ Cup of coconut oil, melted
- 1 Cup of plain greek yogurt
- ¼ Cup of maple syrup
- 2 Eggs
- 1 Tsp. vanilla
- 2 Cups of white whole wheat flour
- ½ Tsp. salt
- ½ Cup of shredded coconut
- 1 Lime, zested
- 2 Cups of cranberries

Cooking Instructions:

1. Begin by Preheating the Air Fryer to 400°F. Line muffin tray with parchment paper. In a small mixing bowl, combine together the yogurt, maple syrup, eggs and vanilla. Stir thoroughly.

2. Put the flour, baking powder, baking soda, salt, coconut and lime zest. Stir thoroughly. Wrap in cranberries.

3. Scoop 3 Tbsp. into each muffin and top each of the muffins with coconut. Place the muffins in the Air Fryer cooking basket and cook for 20 minutes.

4. Check that it is properly cooked before you remove it into a wire rack and allow it to cool totally.

5. Serve and enjoy!!!

Sweet Potato

Preparation Time: 5 minutes

Cooking Time: 35 minutes

Total Time: 40 minutes

Servings: 3

Calories: 153 kcal

Ingredients:

- 1 Tbsp. olive oil
- 3 Sweet potatoes, washed
- 2 Tsp. kosher salt

Cooking Instructions:

1. Begin by Preheating the Air Fryer to 400°F. Using a fork, make air holes in the potatoes. Spray olive oil and salt on the potatoes holes and all over the potatoes.

2. Arrange them in the Air Fryer cooking basket and bake at 390°F for at least 35 minutes. Confirm it is properly cooked.

3. Serve and enjoy!!!

Mushroom with Bruschetta and Goat Cheese

Preparation Time: 15 minutes

Cooking Time: 10 minutes

Total Time: 25 minutes

Servings: 12

Calories: 15 kcal

Ingredients:

- 1 Clove garlic minced
- 1 Tsp. balsamic vinegar
- 12 Fresh whole mushrooms button, washed and stem removed
- 2 Small plum tomatoes
- 2 Tbsp. goat cheese crumbled
- Fresh basil
- Pinch of salt
- Pepper to taste

Cooking Instructions:

1. Start by Preheating the Air Fryer to 400°F. Combine together the tomatoes, garlic and balsamic vinegar in a medium mixing bowl.

2. Pour oil on BBQ vegetable tray and fill the mushroom caps with the bruschetta and place them on the tray.

3. Place in the Air Fryer and cook for 10 minutes. You can now place a small spoonful of goat cheese on the warm bruschetta, spread the basil leaves, and add salt and pepper.

4. Serve and enjoy!!!

Balsamic Roasted Brussels Sprouts

Preparation Time: 10 minutes

Cooking Time: 25 minutes

Total Time: 35 minutes

Servings: 6

Calories: 94 kcal

Ingredients:

- 2 Tbsp. balsamic vinegar
- 1 ½ Lbs. brussels sprouts, washed, stem trimmed off and halved
- 2 Tbsp. olive oil
- Salt
- Pepper

Cooking Instructions:

1. Start by Preheating the Air Fryer to 400°F. In a small mixing bowl, mix together the olive oil, and balsamic vinegar. Toss brussels sprouts on the mixture.

2. Place them on a baking pan. Put salt and pepper. Place in the Air Fryer and cook for 25 minutes turning halfway through the cooking time.

3. Serve and enjoy!!!

Spaghetti Squash

Preparation Time: 2 minutes

Cooking Time: 60 minutes

Total Time: 1 hour 2 minutes

Servings: 4

Calories: 74 kcal

Ingredients:

- 1 Spaghetti squash

Cooking Instructions:

1. Start by Preheating the Air Fryer to 350°F. Lay the spaghetti squash on a baking sheet and poke using a paring knife.

2. Place the baking sheet in the Air Fryer basket and bake for 60 minutes. Remove the squash in half from the middle.

3. Remove seeds and pull the noodles from around the spaghetti using fork.

4. Serve and enjoy!!!

Honey Roasted Carrots

Preparation Time: 5 minutes

Cooking Time: 11 minutes

Total Time: 16 minutes

Servings: 4

Calories: 299 kcal

Ingredients:

1. Salt
2. 3 Cups of baby carrots, chopped
3. 1 Tbsp. Olive oil
4. 1 Tbsp. Honey
5. Pepper

Cooking Instructions:

1. Start by Preheating the Air Fryer to 350°F. Combine together the Carrots, honey and olive oil in a small mixing bowl. Mix well.

2. Put salt and pepper. Place in the Air Fryer cooking basket and cook at 300°F for at least 12 minutes.

3. Serve and enjoy!!!

Nashville Hot Chicken

Preparation Time: 30 minutes

Cooking Time: 10 minutes

Total Time: 40 minutes

Servings: 4

Calories: 413 kcal

Ingredients:

- 2 Tbsp. cayenne pepper
- 2 Tbsp. dark brown sugar
- 2 Tbsp. dill pickle juice, divided
- 2 Tbsp. hot pepper sauce, divided
- 1 Tsp. salt, divided
- 2 Lbs. chicken tenderloins
- 1 Cup of all-purpose flour
- ½ Tsp. pepper
- 1 Large egg
- ½ Cup of buttermilk
- Cooking spray
- ½ Cup of olive oil
- 1 Tsp. paprika
- 1 Tsp. chili powder
- ½ Tsp. garlic powder
- Dill pickle slices

Cooking Instructions:

1. Preheat the Air Fryer to 375°F. Merge together the 1 Tbsp. hot sauce, 1 Tbsp. pickle juice, ½ Tsp. salt, stir well and coat chicken with the mixture.

2. Close and put the mixture in the refrigerator for about an hour. Drain and discard marinade.

3. Combine together flour, the remaining ½ Tsp. salt and pepper in a small mixing bowl.

4. Combine together egg, buttermilk, the remaining 1 Tbsp. pickle juice and 1 Tbsp. hot sauce in another different small mixing bowl.

5. Coat chicken both in the flour and egg mixture respectively. Coat lastly in the four mixtures.

6. Spray cooking oil on baking pan and arrange the chicken on it and then place the pan in Air Fryer cooking basket.

7. Spray with cooking spray again. Cook in the Air Fryer for 6 minutes. Mix together in a small mixing bowl oil, cayenne pepper, brown sugar and seasonings; spread the mixture on top of the chicken.

8. Serve and enjoy!!!

Breaded Mushrooms

Preparation Time: 5 minutes

Cooking Time: 7 minutes

Total Time: 12 minutes

Servings: 2

Calories: 382 kcal

Ingredients:

- Flour
- 1 Egg, beaten
- 250g Button mushrooms, washed and pat dried
- Breadcrumbs
- 80g Grated Parmigiana Reggiano cheese
- Salt to taste
- Pepper to taste

Cooking Instructions:

1. Preheat the Air Fryer to 360°F. Merge together the breadcrumbs and Parmigiana cheese in a small mixing bowl.

2. Roll the mushroom in flour, egg and breadcrumb mixture respectively. Arrange the mushroom in the Air Frye and cook at 360°F shaking the basket halfway through.

3. Serve and enjoy!!!

Frozen Curly Fries

Preparation Time: 5 minutes

Cooking Time: 12 minutes

Total Time: 17 minutes

Servings: 4

Calories: 380 kcal

Ingredients:

- 650g Frozen Curly Fries

Cooking Instructions:

1. Preheat the Air Fryer to 400°F.

2. Arrange the curly fries in the Air Fryer cooking basket and cook for 12 minutes.

3. Serve and enjoy!!!

AIR FRYER VEGAN & VEGETARIAN RECIPES

Sticky Pumpkin Wedges

Preparation Time: 5 minutes

Cooking Time: 25 minutes

Total Time: 30 minutes

Servings: 2

Calories: 285 kcal

Ingredients:

- 1 Lime (juice)
- 1 Tbsp. Balsamic Vinegar
- ½ Medium Pumpkin, sliced into medium size wedges
- 1 Tbsp. Paprika
- 1 Tsp. Turmeric
- Salt
- Pepper

Cooking Instructions:

1. Preheat the Air Fryer to 390°F. Put the pumpkin in a baking pan and place it in the Air Fryer cooking basket. Cook at 370°F for 20 minutes.

2. When the cooking time is up, open the Air Fryer and pour half of your seasonings, vinegar, and lime. Turn them over and put the remaining ingredients.

3. Cook for another 5 minutes. Make ranch dressing available.

4. Serve and enjoy!!!

Flourless Broccoli Cheese Quiche

Preparation Time: 10 minutes

Cooking Time: 40 minutes

Total Time: 50 minutes

Servings: 2

Calories: 488 kcal

Ingredients:

- 150ml Whole Milk
- 2 Large Eggs
- 1 Large Broccoli, chopped into florets
- 3 Large Carrots, peeled and diced
- 1 Large Tomato
- 100g Cheddar Cheese grated
- 20g Feta Cheese
- 1 Tsp. Parsley
- 1 Tsp. Thyme
- Salt
- Pepper

Cooking Instructions:

1. Preheat the Air Fryer to 380°F. Put the carrots and broccoli into a food steamer and cook for at least 20 minutes.

2. Put all the seasoning into a measuring jug, beat eggs into the jug alongside with milk. Whisk thoroughly.

3. Drain the vegetables after the steamer finished steaming and arrange the vegetables on your quiche plate alongside with tomatoes and cheese.

4. Pour the liquid all over and cook in the Air fryer for about 20 minutes.

5. Serve and enjoy!!!

Black Bean Burger

Preparation Time: 10 minutes

Cooking Time: 25 minutes

Total Time: 35 minutes

Servings: 6

Calories: 488 kcal

Ingredients:

- ¾ Cup of salsa
- 1 ¼ Tsp. mild chili powder
- 1 ½ Cups of rolled oats
- 16 Oz. black beans, drained
- ½ Tsp. chipotle chile powder
- ½ Tsp. garlic powder

Cooking Instructions:

1. Preheat the Air Fryer to 375°F. Pulse the oats in a food processor. Put all the ingredients except the corn and pulse again to your desired consistency.

2. Turn the bean mixture into a bowl and add corn. Seal with a cover and place in the refrigerator for at least 15 minutes.

3. Place the burgers in the Air Fryer cooking basket and cook for about 15 minutes.

4. Serve and enjoy!!!

Chocolate Chip Zucchini Bread

Preparation Time: 10 minutes

Cooking Time: 20 minutes

Total Time: 30 minutes

Servings: 4

Calories: 468 kcal

Ingredients:

- 30g Cocoa Powder
- 250ml Olive Oil
- Dieter's Green Tea
- 300g Zucchini, grated
- 385g Self Raising Flour
- 260g Brown Sugar
- 3 Large Eggs
- 200g Dark Chocolate Chips
- 2 Tbsp. Vanilla Essence
- 2 Tsp. Cinnamon
- 1 Tsp. Nutmeg

Cooking Instructions:

1. Preheat the Air fryer to 360°F. Spread the Air Fryer baking pan all over with flour.

2. Merge together the eggs, olive oil, brown sugar and vanilla extract in a large mixing. Stir thoroughly. Fold in the flour, cocoa powder and the green tea.

3. Fold in the grated zucchini and dark chocolate chips. Place the mixture in the Air Fryer cooking basket and then cook at 370°F for at least 20 minutes.

4. Serve and enjoy!!!

Fried Green Tomatoes

Preparation Time: 4 minutes

Cooking Time: 12 minutes

Total Time: 16 minutes

Servings: 4

Calories: 319 kcal

Ingredients:

- 1 Cup of Bobs Red Mill Oat Flour
- 1 Cup of Bobs Red Mill Oat Bran
- 4 Large Green Tomatoes, sliced into medium sizes and dried
- 1 Small Egg
- 1 Cup of Bobs Red Mill Rolled Oats
- 2 Tsp. Paprika
- Salt
- Pepper

Cooking Instructions:

1. Preheat the Air fryer to 390°F. Break the eggs into a small mixing bowl. In another small mixing bowl, merge together the oats, flour, pepper and paprika.

2. Blend half of the rolled oats in a food blender. Put this mixture into another bowl including the oats bran and rolled oats.

3. Add the green tomatoes into the flour bowl, then the egg bowl and finally into the breadcrumbs bowl.

4. Place the mixture in the Air Fryer cooking basket in different batches. Cook at 360°F for about 6 minutes.

5. Serve and enjoy!!!

Rutabaga Fries

Preparation Time: 5 minutes

Cooking Time: 20 minutes

Total Time: 25 minutes

Servings: 2

Calories: 249 kcal

Ingredients:

- 2 Tsp. Thyme
- 1 Kg Rutabaga, peeled and sliced into fries
- 1 Tbsp. Extra Virgin Olive Oil
- Salt
- Pepper

Cooking Instructions:

1. Preheat the Air fryer to 350°F. In a small mixing bowl, put the sliced rutabaga followed by all the ingredients.

2. Mix the ingredients perfectly using your hands. Place the mixture in the Air Fryer cooking basket and cook for 15 minutes.

3. Shake and cook for 5 minutes again.

4. Serve and enjoy!!!

Zucchini Vegetarian Meatballs

Preparation Time: 5 minutes

Cooking Time: 10 minutes

Total Time: 15 minutes

Servings: 4

Calories: 203 kcal

Ingredients:

- 1 Tsp. Lemon Rind
- 6 Basil Leaves thinly sliced
- 2 Cups of Gluten Free Oats
- 150g Zucchini
- 40g Feta Cheese crumbled
- 1 Large Eggs, beaten
- 1 Tsp. Dill
- 1 Tsp. Oregano
- Salt
- Pepper

Cooking Instructions:

1. Preheat the Air Fryer to 400°F. Grate and squeeze out excess water from zucchini into a small bowl and put the zucchini into a mixing bowl alongside with egg.

2. Put the remaining ingredients except the oats. Blend the oats in a food blender to become breadcrumbs.

3. Gradually pour the oats into the bowl for more thickness. Stir well and form small zucchini meatballs. Arrange in the Air Fryer and cook for 10 minutes.

4. Serve and enjoy!!!

Meatless Monday Thai Veggie Bites

Preparation Time: 5 minutes

Cooking Time: 20 minutes

Total Time: 25 minutes

Servings: 16 bites

Calories: 117 kcal

Ingredients:

- 1 Tbsp. Thai Green Curry Paste
- 1 Tbsp. Coriander
- 1 Large Broccoli
- 1 Large Cauliflower
- 6 Large Carrots
- Handful Garden Peas
- ½ Cauliflower made into cauliflower rice
- 1 Large Onion peeled and diced
- 1 Small Courgette
- 2 Leeks cleaned and thinly sliced
- 1 Can Coconut Milk
- 50g Plain Flour
- 1 cm Cube Ginger peeled and grated
- 1 Tbsp. Garlic Puree
- 1 Tbsp. Olive Oil
- 1 Tbsp. Mixed Spice
- 1 Tsp. Cumin
- Salt
- Pepper

Cooking Instructions:

1. Using a wok, cook the onion, garlic, ginger, and olive oil. When the onion is done, put the vegetables into the steamer exception of the courgette and leek.

2. Cook for 20 minutes. Put the courgette, leek and the curry paste into the wok and cook for 5 minutes.

3. Dump in coconut milk and the remaining seasoning and cauliflower rice. Give it a nice mix. Simmer for about 10 minutes and add cooked vegetables.

4. Stir thoroughly and place it in the refrigerator for 1 hour. Cut into bite sizes and arrange them in the Air Fryer cooking basket. Cook for about 10 minutes.

5. Serve and enjoy!!!

Meatless Monday Veggie Bake Cakes

Preparation Time: 2 minutes

Cooking Time: 12 minutes

Total Time: 14 minutes

Servings: 2

Calories: 13 kcal

Ingredients:

- Leftover Vegetable Bake
- 1 Tbsp. Plain Flour

Cooking Instructions:

1. Preheat Air Fryer to 400°F. In order to thicken the leftover vegetable bake, mix it with flour.
2. Pour it into a baking pan and place the pan in the Air Fryer cooking basket. Cook at 350°F for 12 minutes.
3. Serve and enjoy!!!

Vegan Veggie Balls

Preparation Time: 5 minutes

Cooking Time: 12 minutes

Total Time: 17 minutes

Servings: 4

Calories: 212 kcal

Ingredients:

- 100g Sweet Potato
- 70g Carrot
- 1 Tsp. Paprika
- 1 Tsp. Mixed Spice
- 2 Tsp. Oregano
- 200g Cauliflower
- 90g Parsnips
- 2 Tsp. Garlic Puree
- 1 Tsp. Chives
- ½ Cup of Desiccated Coconut
- 1 Cup of Gluten Free Oats
- Salt
- Pepper

Cooking Instructions:

1. Preheat the Air Fryer to 490°F. Drain any excess liquid on the cooked vegetables.

2. Put them in a small mixing bowl, put the seasoning, stir to combine and mould them into small size balls.

3. You can now put them in a refrigerator for 2 hours. Blend coconut and oats in a food blender. Turn into a bowl.

4. Roll the balls in the mixture and lay them in Air Fryer basket. Cook for 10 minutes. Shake the basket and cook for another 2 minutes.

5. Serve and enjoy!!!

Pumpkin French Toast

Preparation Time: 4 minutes

Cooking Time: 16 minutes

Total Time: 20 minutes

Servings: 2

Calories: 210 kcal

Ingredients:

- 3 Tbsp. Whole Milk
- 4 Slices Whole meal Bread
- 1 Small Egg
- 120g Pumpkin, chopped
- 60g Pumpkin Pie Filling
- 2 Tsp. Honey
- Pinch of Nutmeg

Cooking Instructions:

1. Preheat the Air Fryer to 490°F. In a small mixing bowl, merge together the pumpkin, honey and nutmeg.

2. Still thoroughly. Put the pumpkin into the Air Fryer and cook for 8 minutes. Put milk and egg in the pumpkin bowl.

3. Stir thoroughly and put pumpkin pie filling and stir well. Get the pumpkin out from Air Fryer keep at one side. Burry the sliced bread in the mixture.

4. Shake any excess moisture out and put in a baking pan. Place the pan in the Air Fryer basket and cook for 4 minutes.

5. Flip over and continue cooking for another 4 minutes.

6. Serve and enjoy!!!

Pumpkin Bread

Preparation Time: 5 minutes

Cooking Time: 15 minutes

Total Time: 20 minutes

Servings: 4

Calories: 229 kcal

Ingredients:

- 8 Tbsp. Pumpkin Puree
- 6 Tbsp. Gluten Free Oats
- 2 Large Eggs
- 6 Tbsp. Banana Flour
- 4 Tbsp. Greek Yoghurt
- 2 Tbsp. Vanilla Essence
- 4 Tbsp. Honey
- Pinch of Nutmeg

Cooking Instructions:

1. Preheat the Air Fryer to 400°F. Exception of the oats, merge all the ingredients together in medium mixing bowl and stir thoroughly. Stir in oats and mix well.

2. Spread small banana flour on the baking pans and then put the pumpkin bread mixture. Work out the sides to smooth properly.

3. Place the baking pan in the Air Fryer cooking basket and cook for 15 minutes. Cut the sides and edges of the baking pan and remove from the baking pan.

4. Serve and enjoy!!!

AIR FRYER BURGER RECIPES

Bunless Burgers

Preparation Time: 5 minutes

Cooking Time: 20 minutes

Total Time: 25 minutes

Servings: 3

Calories: 190 kcal

Ingredient:

- Handful of Green Beans
- Handful of Lettuce, diced
- Handful of Fresh Thyme, diced
- 400g Minced Beef
- 1 Small Red Onion, diced
- 1 Medium Avocado, peeled and sliced we
- 3 Medium Tomatoes, diced
- 4 Slices Back Bacon
- 1 Tbsp. Tomato Puree
- 1 Tbsp. Olive Oil
- Handful of Fresh Basil, diced
- 1 Tbsp. Parsley
- Salt
- Pepper

Cooking Instructions:

1. Preheat the Air fryer to 360°F. Put the beef, onion, all the seasonings, and tomato puree in a small mixing bowl. Stir well and work out 4 burger shapes.

2. Lay a baking pan in the Air Fryer basket. Lay the burgers on the baking pan and cook for about 10 minutes.

3. Mix together the green beans and olive oil. Add them on top of the burgers. Cook for 5 minutes. Put sliced bacon and for 5 minutes.

4. Immediately the cooking time is up, flip the burgers onto a serving plate and garnish with avocado, bacon, and salad. Serve and enjoy!!!

Leftover Turkey Burgers

Preparation Time: 5 minutes

Cooking Time: 18 minutes

Total Time: 23 minutes

Servings: 4

Calories: 708 kcal

Ingredients:

- 2 Tbsp. Mashed Potato
- 25g Brussel Sprouts, chopped
- 1 Tbsp. Gravy, chopped
- 2 Yorkshire Puddings, chopped
- 30g Cooked Turkey, chopped
- 150g Stuffing
- 100g Cauliflower Cheese, chopped
- 5 Roast Potatoes, chopped
- 5 Roast Parsnips, chopped
- 1 Tsp. Chives, chopped
- 2 Tsp. Parsley, chopped
- Salt
- Pepper

Cooking Instructions:

1. Preheat the Air fryer to 380°F. Put all the ingredients into a large mixing bowl and put in the refrigerator for about 9 hours.

2. Remove and mush everything together using your hands and work out into meatball shapes. Reshape into turkey burger shape.

3. Place in the refrigerator again for an hour. Remove the burgers and arrange them in the Air Fryer basket in batches and cook for 18 minutes.

4. Serve and enjoy!!!

Juicy Cheeseburgers

Preparation Time: 5 minutes

Cooking Time: 15 minutes

Total Time: 20 minutes

Servings: 4

Calories: 281 kcal

Ingredients:

- 1 Tsp. Worcestershire sauce
- 1 ½ Tbsp. Weber Burger Seasoning
- 1 Lb. ground chuck beef
- 1 Tsp. liquid smoke
- Salt
- Pepper
- 4 slices of cheese
- 4 buns

Cooking Instructions:

1. Preheat the Air fryer to 380°F. Merge together the ground beef, liquid smoke, Worcestershire, burger seasoning, salt, and pepper.

2. Make the mixture into 4 burger patties. Lay the burgers in the cooking pan and place in the Air Fryer. Cook for at 360°F for 8 minutes.

3. Turn the burger over to the other side and continue cooking for another 4 minutes. Top with cheese and cook for another 2 minutes.

4. Serve and enjoy!!!

Lentil Burgers

Preparation Time: 10 minutes

Cooking Time: 30 minutes

Total Time: 40 minutes

Servings: 4

Calories: 509 kcal

Ingredients:

- 300g Gluten Free Oats
- 1 Tbsp. Garlic Puree
- 4 Vegan Burger Buns
- 100g Black Beluga Lentils
- 1 Large Carrot peeled and grated
- 1 Large Onion peeled and diced
- 100g White Cabbage
- 1 Tsp. Cumin
- Handful Fresh Basil, chopped
- Salt
- Pepper

Cooking Instructions:

1. Preheat the Air fryer to 380°F. Blend oats in a food blender. Put the lentils in a saucepan, fill the pan with water and cook for about 45 minutes.

2. Drain the lentils and put in a small mixing bowl alongside with steamed vegetables and oats.

3. Put seasoning and work the mixture out burgers. Lay them in the Air Fryer basket and cook for about 30 minutes. Top with salad and began mayonnaise.

4. Serve and enjoy!!!

Falafel Burger

Preparation Time: 3 minutes

Cooking Time: 15 minutes

Total Time: 18 minutes

Servings: 2

Calories: 709 kcal

Ingredients:

- 4 Tbsp. Soft Cheese
- 1 Tbsp. Garlic Puree
- 1 Tbsp. Coriander
- 400g Can Chickpeas, drained
- 1 Small Red Onion
- 1 Small Lemon, juice
- 140g Gluten Free Oats
- 28g Cheese
- 28g Feta Cheese
- 3 Tbsp. Greek Yoghurt
- 1 Tbsp. Oregano
- 1 Tbsp. Parsley
- Salt
- Pepper

Cooking Instructions:

1. Preheat the Air fryer to 400°F. Dump all the seasoning into a food blender alongside with the red onion, garlic, lemon rind, and chickpeas. Mix well.

2. Turn into a bowl and add half of feta, soft and hard cheese. Work out to burger shapes. Roll the burgers in oats and put them in a baking pan.

3. Place the pan in the Air Fryer cooking basket and cook for 8 minutes. Merge together the soft cheese, Greek Yoghurt, salt and pepper in a bowl.

4. Give the mixture a good mix until you have a fluffy surface. Put lemon juice give the mixture a thorough stir.

5. Lay the falafel burger in the homemade buns with garnish. Serve and enjoy!!!

Hamburgers

Preparation Time: 10 minutes

Cooking Time: 16 minutes

Total Time: 26 minutes

Servings: 4

Calories: 325 kcal

Ingredients:

- 1 Tsp. salt
- 1 Tsp. garlic powder
- 1 Lb. ground beef
- 1 Tsp. onion powder
- ¼ Tsp. black pepper
- 1 Tsp. Worcestershire sauce
- 4 burger buns

Cooking Instructions:

1. Preheat the Air fryer to 360°F. In a small mixing bowl, merge together the beef, seasoning and mix the mixture using your hand. Roll it to a ball shape.

2. Equally divide the ball into 4 parts. Form patties from each of the parts. Put the patties in a baking pan.

3. Lay it in the Air Fryer basket and cook for 16 minutes. Turning halfway through the cooking time.

4. Serve and enjoy!!!

KFC Zinger Chicken Burger

Preparation Time: 10 minutes

Cooking Time: 15 minutes

Total Time: 25 minutes

Servings: 4

Calories: 549 kcal

Ingredients:

- 100ml Bread Crumbs
- 1 Tsp. Worcester Sauce
- 6 Chicken Breasts, minced
- 1 Small Egg beaten
- 50g Plain Flour
- 10ml KFC Spice Blend
- 1 Tsp. Mustard Powder
- 1 Tsp. Paprika
- Salt
- Pepper

Cooking Instructions:

1. Merge together the Worcester sauce, mustard, paprika and salt and pepper in a food blender and blend well. Work out the chicken into burger shapes.

2. Beat egg into a small mixing bowl, put flour another small mixing bowl and then KFC spice blend alongside with breadcrumbs in another bowl.

3. Cover the burgers in the flour, egg and bread crumbs respectively. Place it in the Air Fryer basket and cook for 15 minutes. Check for doneness.

4. Serve and enjoy!!!

Portobello Burger with Basil Pesto-mayo

Preparation Time: 5 minutes

Cooking Time: 7 minutes

Total Time: 12 minutes

Servings: 2

Calories: 299 kcal

Ingredients:

- 2 Ciabatta buns grilled
- 1 Roma tomato sliced
- ¼ Cup of balsamic vinegar
- ¼ Cup of olive oil
- 2 Tbsp. lemon juice
- 1 Tbsp. Dijon mustard
- ½ Tsp. Kosher salt
- 2 Portobello mushroom caps, stems removed
- 2 Cups of fresh spinach, sautéed
- ½ Red onion thinly sliced
- 1 Cup of basil pesto
- 2 Tbsp. mayo

Cooking Instructions:

1. Preheat the Air Fryer to 400°F. Merge together the balsamic vinegar, olive oil, lemon juice, mustard, and salt in a small mixing bowl.

2. Use a sealable bag and put the mushroom. Pour in marinade, seal bag, and mix well. Allow it to marinate for 30 minutes.

3. Put them in the Air Fryer basket and cook at 370°F for 7 minutes. Merge together pesto and mayo spread on toasted bun.

4. When the cooking cycle is over, flip the mushroom onto a plate and keep for sometimes.

5. You can build your burger to your own likeness. Make sure it is properly cooked.

6. Serve and enjoy!!!

Gourmet Blue Cheese Burgers

Preparation Time: 10 minutes

Cooking Time: 6 minutes

Total Time: 16 minutes

Servings: 4

Calories: 260 kcal

Ingredients:

- ¼ Tsp. hot pepper sauce
- 1 Tsp. Worcestershire sauce
- 3 Lbs. lean ground meat
- 4 Oz. blue cheese
- ⅛ Cup of minced fresh chives
- 1 Tsp. black pepper
- 1 Tsp. salt
- 1 Tsp. dry mustard
- 12 Brioche hamburger rolls

Cooking Instructions:

1. Preheat Air Fryer to 370°F. Combine together the chives, meat, blue cheese, hot pepper sauce, Worcestershire sauce, salt and pepper.

2. Dry mustard in a small mixing bowl. Close the bowl of the mixture properly and put in the refrigerator for at least an hour. This will enable the meat to firm up.

3. Form the mixture into patties. Lay them in the Air Fryer basket and cook for 6 minutes turning halfway cooking time.

4. Serve and enjoy!!!

Lamb Burgers

Preparation Time: 3 minutes

Cooking Time: 18 minutes

Total Time: 21 minutes

Servings: 4

Calories: 478 kcal

Ingredients:

- 1 Tsp. Harissa Paste
- 1 Tbsp. Moroccan Spice
- 650g Minced Lamb
- 2 Tsp. Garlic Puree
- Salt
- Pepper
- Greek Dip:
- 3 Tbsp. Greek Yoghurt
- 1 Tsp. Moroccan Spice
- ½ Tsp. Oregano
- 1 Small Lemon, juice

Cooking Instructions:

1. Preheat the Air Fryer to 400°F. Combine together the first six ingredients in a small mixing bowl. Give it a nice stir.

2. Work out the mixture into lamb burger shapes. Arrange them in the Air Fryer cooking basket and cook for about 18 minutes.

3. When the burgers are yet to be completely cooked, prepare the Greek Dip. Merge together the Greek Dip ingredients using a fork. Stir well.

4. Serve and enjoy!!!!

AIR FRYER APPETIZER RECIPES

Asparagus Fries

Preparation Time: 10 minutes

Cooking Time: 7 minutes

Total Time: 17 minutes

Servings: 4

Calories: 362 kcal

Ingredients:

- 1 Lb. asparagus spears, trimmed, rinsed and pat dried
- 1 Cup of Italian style breadcrumbs
- ½ Tsp. garlic powder
- ¼ Tsp. salt
- ¼ Tsp. black pepper
- ½ Cup of all-purpose flour
- 2 Large eggs, beaten

Cooking Instructions:

1. Preheat the Air Fryer to 400°F. In a small mixing bowl, merge together the breadcrumbs, garlic powder, salt and pepper.

2. Dredge the asparagus spears in the flour; put it in the beaten eggs and then breadcrumbs respectively.

3. Arrange them in the baking pan and lay the pan in the Air Fryer basket. Cook at 400°F for 7 minutes.

4. Serve and enjoy!!!

Banana Bread

Preparation Time: 10 minutes

Cooking Time: 35 minutes

Total Time: 45 minutes

Servings: 8

Calories: 338 kcal

Ingredients:

- 2 Large eggs, beaten
- ½ Cup of granulated sugar
- ⅓ Cup of plain nonfat yogurt
- ¾ Cup of white-whole wheat flour
- 1 Tsp. cinnamon
- ½ Tsp. Kosher salt
- ¼ Tsp. Baking soda
- 2 Medium ripe bananas, mashed
- 2 Tbsp. vegetable oil
- 1 Tsp. Vanilla extract
- 2 Tbsp. toasted walnuts, chopped
- Cooking spray

Cooking Instructions:

1. Preheat the Air Fryer to 390°F. Arrange parchment paper in a baking pan and wet the pan with cooking spray.

2. In a small mixing bowl, combine together the flour, cinnamon, salt and baking soda. Stir well.

3. Combine together the sugar, eggs, mashed bananas, yogurt, oil and vanilla in another small mixing bowl.

4. Turn over wet ingredients into flour mixture. Mix well and spread the mixture in the baking pan. Top with walnuts.

5. Place the cooking pan in the Air Fryer cooking basket and cook at 310°F for 35 minutes, turning the pan halfway through the cooking cycle.

6. Flip the bread on to a wire rack and allow it to cool.

7. Serve and enjoy!!!

Cheesy Garlic Bread

Preparation Time: 10 minutes

Cooking Time: 7 minutes

Total Time: 17 minutes

Servings: 2

Calories: 421 kcal

Ingredients:

- 2 Tsp. garlic powder
- Sea salt
- 1 French baguette loaf, divided into 3 and cut into rectangles (lenghtwise)
- ¼ Cup of butter, softened
- Freshly ground black pepper
- ¾ Cup of shredded Cheddar cheese
- ¼ Cup of shredded mozzarella cheese
- Parsley, chopped

Cooking Instructions:

1. Preheat Air Fryer to 400°F. Apply the butter, garlic powder, salt and pepper on the inside of the bread slices.

2. Apply Cheddar cheese and mozzarella cheese over butter and seasoning mixture on each slice of the bread.

3. Arrange them in a baking pan and place the pan in the Air Fryer cooking basket. Cook for 7 minutes. Garnish with parsley.

4. Serve and enjoy!!!

Corn Nuts

Preparation Time: 10 minutes

Cooking Time: 25 minutes

Total Time: 35 minutes

Servings: 8

Calories: 225 kcal

Ingredients:

- 14 Oz. giant white corn, soaked for 8 hours
- 3 Tbsp. vegetable oil
- 1 ½ Tsp. salt

Cooking Instructions:

1. Preheat Air Fryer to 400°F. Drain the soaked corn into a large baking pan. Allow it to dry completely. In a large mixing bowl, put the corn, oil and salt. Mix well.

2. Place the corn in the Air Fryer basket and cook for 10 minutes shaking basket twice and cooking for 10 and 5 minutes respectively.

3. Flip onto a plate lined with paper towel.

4. Serve and enjoy!!!

Air Fryer Donut

Preparation Time: 2 hours 15 minutes

Cooking Time: 5 minutes

Total Time: 2 hours 20 minutes

Servings: 16

Calories: 225 kcal

Ingredients:

- Powdered sugar
- 4 Frozen Rhodes Yeast Dinner Rolls
- 4 Tbsp. Butter, melted
- 3 Tbsp. Sugar mixed with 1 Tbsp. Cinnamon

Cooking Instructions:

1. Preheat Air Fryer to 400°F. Place the Rhodes in a greased baking pan. Close with plastic wrap. Keep it in a warm place that is free of draft for 3 hours.

2. Remove the dough and divide into 4 equal places using a scissors. Burry into the butter and cinnamon sugar respectively.

3. Lay the baking pan in the Air Fryer basket and cook in batches for 5 minutes. Confirm that it is well cooked. Top with more powdered sugar.

4. Serve and enjoy!!!

Shishito Peppers

Preparation Time: 5 minutes

Cooking Time: 5 minutes

Total Time: 10 minutes

Servings: 2

Calories: 21 kcal

Ingredients:

- 1 Dry pint shish to peppers
- Cooking spray
- Salt

Cooking Instructions:

1. Preheat Air Fryer to 400°F. Arrange the pepper in the Air Fryer basket and spray the cooking spray. Shake the basket.

2. Cook for 5 minutes shaking the basket halfway through cooking cycle. Flip the peppers onto a serving plate and apply salt.

3. Serve and enjoy!!!

Spicy Roasted Peanuts

Preparation Time: 5 minutes

Cooking Time: 25 minutes

Total Time: 30 minutes

Servings: 2

Calories: 219 kcal

Ingredients:

- 2 Tbsp. olive oil
- 3 Tsp. seafood seasoning
- ½ Tsp. pepper
- 8 Oz. Raw Spanish peanuts
- Salt

Cooking Instructions:

1. Preheat Air Fryer to 320°F. I'm a medium mixing bowl, combine together the olive oil, seafood seasoning, cayenne pepper, peanuts and mix thoroughly.

2. Arrange peanut in the Air Fryer basket and cook for 10 minutes. Shake the basket and cook for another 10 minutes.

3. Remove the Air Fryer basket and sprinkle salt on the peanuts. Toss and cook again for 5 minutes.

4. Serve and enjoy!!!

Tempura Veggies

Preparation Time: 15 minutes

Cooking Time: 20 minutes

Total Time: 35 minutes

Servings: 4

Calories: 247 kcal

Ingredients:

- ½ Cup of whole green beans
- ½ Cup of whole asparagus spears
- ½ Cup of all-purpose flour
- ½ Tsp. salt
- ½ Tsp. ground black pepper
- 2 Eggs
- 2 Tbsp. water
- 1 Cup of panko bread crumbs
- 2 Tsp. vegetable oil
- ½ Cup of red onion rings
- ½ Cup of sweet pepper rings
- ½ Cup of avocado wedges
- ½ Cup of zucchini slices

Cooking Instructions:

1. Preheat Air Fryer to 400°F. In a small mixing bowl, combine together the flour, ¼ Tsp. salt, and pepper.

2. In another small mixing bowl, combine together the eggs and water. In another separate small mixing bowl, mix panko and oil.

3. Stir in seasoning of your choice to flour and panko mixture. Apply the remaining salt on the vegetables.

4. Dump in flour mixture, egg mixture, and panko mixture respectively. Working in batches, arrange the vegetables in the Air Fryer basket.

5. Cook at 320°F for 10 minutes. Do these for the remaining vegetables.

6. Serve and enjoy!!!

Potato Hay

Preparation Time: 10 minutes

Cooking Time: 30 minutes

Total Time: 40 minutes

Servings: 2

Calories: 113 kcal

Ingredients:

- 2 Russet potatoes, cut into spirals
- 1 Tbsp. canola oil
- Kosher salt
- Ground black pepper

Cooking Instructions:

1. Preheat Air Fryer to 400°F. Cut the potato spirals with kitchen shears. Put water in a bowl and soak the potatoes for 20 minutes.

2. Drain and pat dry with paper towels. Put the potatoes in a plastic bag. Pour in salt, oil and pepper.

3. Working in batches, arrange the potatoes in the Air Fryer basket and cook for 5 minutes.

4. Shake the basket and cook again for another 10 minutes. Do these for remaining potatoes.

5. Serve and enjoy!!!

Honey Garlic Chicken Wings

Preparation Time: 5 minutes

Cooking Time: 20 minutes

Total Time: 25 minutes

Servings: 8

Calories: 113 kcal

Ingredients:

- ¼ Cup of potato starch
- 3 cloves garlic
- 1 ½ Lbs. chicken wings
- 2 Tbsp. soy sauce
- 1 Tbsp. butter
- 3 Tbsp. honey
- ½ Tsp. salt
- 1 Tsp. red pepper flakes

Cooking Instructions:

1. Preheat Air Fryer to 400°F. Mix together chicken wings and soy sauce. Place the potato starch in a large zip top plastic bag and put chicken wings to bag.

2. Give it a good shake for everything to mix properly. Sprinkle oil in the Air Fryer bask. Place the chicken wings in the basket.

3. Working in batches, cook the wings at 360°F for 12 minutes. Turn over to the other side and cook for another 17 minutes.

4. Meanwhile microwave garlic and butter for 30 seconds. Put honey, salt and red pepper flakes. Toss wings in sauce.

5. Serve and enjoy!!!

Fried Pickles

Preparation Time: 10 minutes

Cooking Time: 20 minutes

Total Time: 30 minutes

Servings: 8

Calories: 65 kcal

Ingredients:

- 1 Tsp. paprika
- ½ Tsp. salt
- ¾ Cup of panko bread crumbs
- 1 Tsp. dried oregano
- 1 Tsp. garlic powder
- ¼ Tsp. pepper
- 1 Egg
- 1 Jar dill pickle slices
- Ranch

Cooking Instructions:

1. Preheat Air Fryer to 400°F. Sprinkle cooking oil on the Air Fryer basket. Merge together the oregano, panko, garlic powder, paprika, salt and pepper.

2. Beat the egg into a small mixing bowl. Pat pickles the chips and dry with paper towels. Dump the chips in the egg and breadcrumb mixture respectively.

3. Working in batches, arrange the pickle chips in the Air Fryer cooking basket and cook at 380°F for 5 minutes. Make your favorite sauce available.

4. Serve and enjoy!!!

Chinese Garlic Chicken

Preparation Time: 10 minutes

Cooking Time: 5 minutes

Total Time: 15 minutes

Servings: 4

Calories: 363 kcal

Ingredients:

- ¼ Cup of soy sauce
- 1 Tbsp. sesame oil
- 5 Cloves of garlic, minced
- 2 Tbsp. honey
- 1 Tbsp. cornstarch
- 1 Tbsp. vegetable oil
- 1 Lb. chicken breast, sliced into small pieces

Cooking Instructions:

1. Preheat Air Fryer to 400°F. In a small mixing bowl, combine together the garlic, soy sauce, sesame oil, honey and cornstarch. Stir thoroughly.

2. Sprinkle oil in the Air Fryer basket. Arrange chicken and the garlic mixture into a baking pan. Place the pan in the Air Fryer basket and cook for 5 minutes.

3. Serve and enjoy!!!

AIR FRYER DESSERT RECIPES

Cashew Chocolate Brownies

Preparation Time: 5 minutes

Cooking Time: 18 minutes

Total Time: 23 minutes

Servings: 9

Calories: 344 kcal

Ingredients:

- Alchemy gluten-free chocolate brownie mix
- 100g Butter melted
- 2 Large eggs beaten
- 55g roasted cashew nuts, chopped

Cooking Instructions:

1. Preheat Air Fryer to 350°F. Mix together the brownie mix and butter in a small mixing bowl. Add eggs and cashew. Stir thoroughly.

2. Put the mixture in a baking pan. Place the pan in the Air Fryer basket and cook for about 18 minutes.

3. Serve and enjoy!!!

Apple Pie Egg Rolls

Preparation Time: 25 minutes

Cooking Time: 15 minutes

Total Time: 40 minutes

Servings: 8

Calories: 273 kcal

Ingredients:

- 8 Egg roll wrappers
- ½ Cup of spreadable cream cheese
- 3 Cups of tart apples, peeled and chopped
- ½ Cup of packed light brown sugar
- 2 ½ Tsp. ground cinnamon, divided
- 1 Tsp. corn starch
- Cooking spray
- 1 Tbsp. sugar
- ⅔ Cup of hot caramel ice cream

Cooking Instructions:

1. Preheat Air Fryer to 400°F. Mix together the brown sugar, apples, 2 Tsp. cinnamon and corn starch.

2. Spread 1 scant Tbsp. cream cheese within 1 inch at the edges. Pour ⅓ cup of apple mixture center of wrapper. Fold bottom corner over filling.

3. Sprinkle water on the remaining wrapper edges. Wrap side corners toward center over filling. You can now roll egg roll up very tight.

4. Seal it by pressing the tip. Grease baking pan with oil. Arrange the egg rolls in the pan and place it in the Air Fryer basket. Spray with the cooking spray.

5. Cook at 400°F for 5 minutes. Flip the egg roll over and cook for another 5 minutes. Mix sugar and remaining ½ Tsp. cinnamon.

6. Place and roll egg rolls in the mixture. Serve and enjoy!!!

Chocolate Chip Oatmeal Cookies

Preparation Time: 20 minutes

Cooking Time: 10 minutes

Total Time: 30 minutes

Servings: 6

Calories: 102 kcal

Ingredients:

- 3 Cups of quick-cooking oats
- 1 ½ Cups of all-purpose flour
- 1 Package instant vanilla pudding mix
- 1 Cup of butter, softened
- ¾ Cup of sugar
- ¾ Cup of packed brown sugar
- 2 Large eggs, room temperature
- 1 Tsp. vanilla extract
- 1 Tsp. baking soda
- 1 Tsp. salt
- 2 Cups of semi-sweet chocolate chips
- 1 Cup nuts

Cooking Instructions:

1. Preheat Air Fryer to 400°F. Merge together the sugars, cream butter, egg and vanilla in a small mixing bowl.

2. Combine together the oats, flour, dry pudding mix, baking soda and salt in another small mixing bowl. Stir it into egg mixture.

3. Add chocolate chips and nuts. Place dough by Tbsp. into a baking pan; flatten tje dough. Place the dough in the baking pan and place in the Air Fryer basket. Cook for 10 minutes.

4. Serve and enjoy!!!

Apple Chips

Preparation Time: 10 minutes

Cooking Time: 20 minutes

Total Time: 30 minutes

Servings: 2

Calories: 48 kcal

Ingredients:

- 1 Apple, sliced
- ¼ Tsp. ground cinnamon
- Pinch of salt

Cooking Instructions:

1. Preheat Air Fryer to 400°F. In a small mixing bowl, merge together apples, cinnamon and salt.

2. Place about half of the apples in the Air Fryer basket. Cook for 10 minutes.

3. Flip over, flatten and cook again for another 10 minutes.

4. Serve and enjoy!!!

Zebra Butter Cake

Preparation Time: 10 minutes

Cooking Time: 30 minutes

Total Time: 40 minutes

Servings: 6

Calories: 319 kcal

Ingredients:

- 115g Butter
- 2 Eggs
- 100g Castor sugar
- 100g Self raising flour, sifted
- 30ml Milk
- 1 Tsp. vanilla extract
- 1 Tbsp. of cocoa powder

Cooking Instructions:

1. Preheat Air Fryer to 360°F. Line parchment paper on a tin base and sprinkle oil on the sides of the tin.

2. Put butter, sugar, eggs, vanilla extract, and milk in a mixing bowl. Pour flour, mix and spoon half of the mixture and keep aside.

3. Put cocoa powder and stir thoroughly. Spoon 2 Tbsp. of the plain mixture onto the middle of the baking tin.

4. Place 2 Tbsp. chocolate mixture on the center of plain mixture on tin. Repeat this step till the mixture finish.

5. Tap or hit the tin for evenly spread of the batter. Arrange them in the Air Fryer basket and cook at 380°F for 30 minutes.

6. Serve and enjoy!!!

Strawberry Cheesecake Egg Rolls

Preparation Time: 5 minutes

Cooking Time: 10 minutes

Total Time: 15 minutes

Servings: 12

Calories: 288 kcal

Ingredients:

- ½ Cup of sour cream
- 1 Tsp. of vanilla extract
- 8 Oz. of softened cream cheese
- ½ Cup of sugar
- 1 Cup of fresh strawberries, diced
- 12 Egg roll wrappers
- Cooking spray
- Confectioner's sugar

Cooking Instructions:

1. Preheat Air Fryer to 380°F. In a mixing bowl, combine together the cream cheese, sugar, sour cream and vanilla extract.

2. Remove the egg roll wrappers and put a Tbsp. of cream cheese mixture to the middle. Place strawberries on the top.

3. From the edge, fold the wrapper and fold the sides too. Firmly roll the egg roll and close with some drops of water.

4. Sprinkle cooking spray on the egg roll and arrange them in the Air Fryer basket. Cook for 10 minutes. Garnish with confectioner's sugar and strawberries.

5. Serve and enjoy!!!

Campfire Nutella Smores

Preparation Time: 2 minutes

Cooking Time: 5 minutes

Total Time: 7 minutes

Servings: 4

Calories: 172 kcal

Ingredients:

- Strawberries
- 4 Graham crackers, halved
- 4 Jumbo marshmallows
- Raspberries
- 4 Tsp. of Nutella

Cooking Instructions:

1. Preheat Air Fryer to 380°F. Lay the 4 graham crackers in the Air Fryer basket, placing 1 marshmallow on top of each of the crackers.

2. Cook at 380°F for 5 minutes. Put the berries and the Nutella placing a graham cracker half on the top.

3. Serve and enjoy!!!

Shortbread

Preparation Time: 10 minutes

Cooking Time: 10 minutes

Total Time: 20 minutes

Servings: 4

Calories: 635 kcal

Ingredients:

1. 250g Self Raising Flour
2. 175g Butter
3. 75g Caster Sugar

Cooking Instructions:

1. Preheat Air Fryer to 380°F. Combine together butter, self-raising flour, and caster sugar. Give it a nice stir.

2. Work it out to short bread dough and roll it using a rolling pin. Cut the dough to your desired shapes.

3. Place the dough in a baking pan and put the pan in the Air Fryer basket. Cook for 10 minutes.

4. Serve and enjoy!!!

Chocolate Cake

Preparation Time: 10 minutes

Cooking Time: 30 minutes

Total Time: 40 minutes

Servings: 4

Calories: 573 kcal

Ingredients:

- ⅔ Cup of sugar
- 1 Stick butter
- 3 Eggs
- ½ Cup of sour cream
- 1 Cup of flour
- ⅓ Cup of cocoa powder
- 1 Tsp. baking powder
- ½ Tsp. baking soda
- 2 Tsp. vanilla

Cooking Instructions:

1. Preheat Air Fryer to 320°F. In a small mixing bowl, combine all the ingredients together and give it a good stir.

2. Place the mixture in a baking pan and lay the pan in the Air Fryer basket. Cook for 30 minutes.

3. Flip onto a serving plate. Top with your favorite chocolate frosting.

4. Serve and enjoy!!!

Midnight Nutella Banana Sandwich

Preparation Time: 5 minutes

Cooking Time: 8 minutes

Total Time: 13 minutes

Servings: 2

Calories: 345 kcal

Ingredients:

- Butter, softened
- 4 Slices white bread
- ¼ Cup of chocolate hazelnut spread Nutella
- 1 Banana, halved

Cooking Instructions:

1. Preheat Air Fryer to 370°F. Apply butter on one side of the bread and set aside. Apply chocolate hazelnut on the other side of the bread.

2. Cut each half of the banana into 3 (lengthwise). Lay the banana on 2 slices of bread and place the remaining 2 slices of bread on top. Cut the sandwich into 2.

3. Place the sandwiches in the Air Fryer baking pan and put the pan in the Air Fryer basket. Bake for 5 minutes. Turnover and bake for 3 minutes again.

4. Serve and enjoy!!!

Air Baked Molten Lava Cakes

Preparation Time: 10 minutes

Cooking Time: 10 minutes

Total Time: 20 minutes

Servings: 4

Calories: 418 kcal

Ingredients:

- ¾ Oz. Unsalted Butter, melted
- ½ Tbsp. Self-Rising Flour
- ¾ Tbsp. Baker's Sugar
- ¾ Oz. Dark Chocolate, Chopped and melted
- 2 Eggs

Cooking Instructions:

1. Preheat Air Fryer to 375°F. Sprinkle oil and flour on 4 ramekins. Combine eggs and sugar together in a bowl.

2. Add chocolate mixture into egg mixture and put flour. Stir it thoroughly. Put into the 4 ramekins. Place in the Air Fryer and cook for 10 minutes.

3. Remove and allow the cake to cool off. Flip the cake on to a serving plate. You can top with raspberry.

4. Serve and enjoy!!!

www.ingramcontent.com/pod-product-compliance
Lightning Source LLC
Chambersburg PA
CEHW081747100526
44592CB00015B/2332